1885

BEER AND
BREWING VOL. 7

1987 TRANSCRIPTS

BEER AND BREWING VOL. 7

17 CHAPTERS ON BREWING BY
- ◀ DR. GEORGE FIX
- ◀ JIM KOCH
- ◀ BYRON BURCH
- ◀ FINN KNUDSEN
- ◀ MARK CARPENTER
- ◀ CHARLIE PAPAZIAN
- ◀ DEWAYNE LEE SAXTON
- ◀ PLUS TEN OTHERS

NATIONAL CONFERENCE
FOR QUALITY BEER AND BREWING

The "Year of the Beer" Edition
Edited by Virginia Thomas

Brewers Publications

Beer and Brewing, Vol. 7
Edited by Virginia Thomas
Copyright © 1987 by Association of Brewers

ISBN 0-937381-07-1
Printed in the United States of America

Published by Brewers Publications
a division of the Association of Brewers
P.O. Box 287, Boulder, Colorado 80306 USA
Tel. 303-447-0816

Direct all inquiries/orders to the above address.

Cover designed by David Bjorkman
Interior Photos by David Bjorkman, National News Service

Contents

Acknowledgments

Special thanks to the following companies who assisted financially in the production of this book:

Anchor Brewing Company,
San Francisco, California

Anheuser-Busch, Inc.,
St. Louis, Missouri

Boston Beer Company,
Jamaica Plain, Massachusetts

Brick Brewing Company,
Waterloo, Ontario, Canada

Koolau Brewery,
Honolulu, Hawaii

Participants in the 1987 National Conference on Quality Beer and Brewing, Denver, Colorado.

Foreword

The seventeen chapters included in this book were presented originally as talks at the Conference for Quality Beer and Brewing in Denver, Colorado, in June 1987. Transforming these presentations into this volume on brewing is one of the most satisfying projects we do here at Brewers Publications for two reasons in particular.

First, as editor of this book, I particularly enjoy working with the material unique to each speaker. In every case, I try to preserve the flavor, the enthusiasm and the character of each individual, while changing the spoken word into the written word (an almost completely different form of the English language.) Of course, accuracy is paramount, and in almost every case, the authors have read their talks after transcription and made changes and additions.

Second, I like the project because it offers the reader such a wide perspective on brewing: from the historical observations of Kihm Winship and Will Anderson; to the technical advice of Dr. George Fix and Jim Koch; to the commercial considerations of Jon Bove, Geoffrey Larson,

Dewayne Saxton, and Finn Knudsen; to the beer enjoyment tips of Mark Carpenter, Charlie Papazian and Michael Jackson. What other volume on brewing covers this variety of topics?

I wish to thank David Bjorkman, National News Service photographer, for contributing to this book his photos of the authors.

I also thank Lois Canaday for her meticulous proofreading.

Virginia Thomas

And I thank the authors not only for presenting their speeches at the Conference, but also for caring enough to then correct the written copy that appears here.

Virginia Thomas
Boulder, Colorado

1.
Perceiving Flavor
Techniques for Recognizing Beer's Subtle Flavor Components

Jim Koch
Boston Beer Company, Boston, Mass.

First, I will speak about my views on flavor in beer, particularly in lager. While my views are very personal, they also are empirical and objective because I don't have a great palate and so I must work from data as well as taste.

Then, we will study four different paired sets of beer: eight beers in total.

Flavor Profile of Beer

I will start with the basics — which in talking about beer, means malt and hops. To me, these are the heart and soul of beer flavor. Beer is fundamentally a combination of the sweetness and body of the malt — that is the heart; and the spiceness and bitterness of the hops — the soul. Of course, there are other major variables, such as the use of caramel or black malt, the fermentation temperatures, the type of hops used, the timing of adding the hops, and infinite minor variables. But to me, of first importance are the malt and the hops.

1

I believe malt and hops are so important that they shed light on beer styles in an objective way. But to do that, the malt and hop content must be measured in a quantifiable way. Hop content is fairly straightforward: it is normally measured in International Bitterness Units (IBU). One IBU is one part per million of isohumulones in the beer. IBUs actually measure something slightly different from simple

Jim Koch

bitterness. This is because really good hops produce isohumulones that don't taste so starkly bitter, while cheap hops produce very bitter isohumulones.

There are other components of hop flavor besides simple bitterness. Hops added early in the boil produce more bitter taste at the same IBU level than hops added later. And I think the same thing is true of hop extract: it tastes more bitter at the same IBU level.

Malt content can be measured in several ways such as original gravity, real extract, and apparent extract. I believe that what you really taste and feel in your mouth is best measured as apparent extract. The malt content in finished beer can be measured with a saccharometer. The saccharometer reading in finished beer is the apparent extract.

Actually, a saccharometer is a very useful tool. Most homebrewers don't utilize its potential, but remember that is just about the only tool all brewers had for many years. For example, the saccharometer is all that is needed to measure alcohol, real extract and calories in beer. To do this, take the original gravity and subtract the apparent extract. Then multiply that figure by 0.43, which will give the approximate alcohol by weight of the beer:

Original Gravity - Apparent Extract x 0.43 =
Alcohol by Weight

For example:
OG - AE x 0.43 = Alcohol by Weight

An OG of 12.0 and an AE of 2.0 would yield:
12.0 - 2.0 x 0.43 = 4.3 Alcohol w/w

You can also figure the real extract of beer: take the apparent extract and add the alcohol by weight multiplied by 0.46. This shows the approximate real extract (the actual amount of solids in the beer). Apparent extract is lower because the alcohol lowers the specific gravity.

Apparent Extract + (Alcohol by Weight x 0.46) =
Real Extract

For example:
AE + (Alcohol w/w x 0.46) = RE

An AE of 2.0 and alcohol of 4.3 (from the example above) would yield:
2.0 + (4.3 x 0.46) = 3.98 Real Extract

You can even use the saccharometer and these formulas to figure the calories in beer. Take the real extract and multiply it by 14, then add the alcohol by weight multiplied by 24. To this, add approximately 5 for the protein in an adjunct brew and 8 in an all-malt brewery, and you have the approximate calories. (These calculations use rule-of-thumb constants, but are accurate within 5 percent in virtually all cases.)

$$(\text{Real Extract} \times 14) + (\text{Alcohol by Weight} \times 24) + 5.0 = \text{Calories}$$

$$(3.98 \times 14) + (4.3 \times 24) + 5 = 164 \text{ calories}$$

From this you see that a saccharometer is a very useful tool. You can figure the original gravity, the apparent extract, the real extract, and the calories of beer. But of these, the apparent extract is what really identifies the malt that you sense in your mouth.

I have analyzed almost thirty beers for a number of characteristics, including the relationship between the apparent extract and bitterness. Although I can't authorize that the data I am presenting here be printed in the transcript since it is proprietary information, this relationship is crucial for understanding the structure of beer flavor.

On the horizontal axis, I rate apparent extract, which means more body. On the vertical axis, I rate International Bitterness Units. There is a strong relationship between the two: beers have a characteristic structure. Within the universe of lagers (I don't know about ales), there is a very characteristic set of relationships between apparent extract and IBUs. I have observed that 80 to 90 percent of the beers sold in America are all within a very

Jim Koch directs tasting of his samples.

limited range, particularly with respect to apparent extract of 10 to 15 IBUs and below 2.5 percent apparent extract. These are the premium beers: the Buds, Millers, Stroh's, Coors, Special Exports, and the light beers.

Then when Americans want something different, they drink Corona or Molson (around 2.2 percent apparent extract and 15 IBUs), which have a little more body and a little more bitterness. Some brewers keep the same amount of body, but go up the bitterness scale, like Heineken or the Beck's beer sold in the U.S. (approximately the same apparent extract, but 20 to 25 IBUs). Beck's German version is very different. This category, together with the first category, is probably 97 percent of the beer consumed in this country

You also have to remember that the beer recipes in American breweries evolve. My grandfather worked for one of today's major breweries, and his job was to reformulate slightly the beers every couple of years. This has been true for fifty years, and the latest incident was when several major breweries had a problem with the hops supply last year.

Samuel Adams is very similar to Pilsner Urquell (at over 30 IBUs and over 4.0 percent apparent extract), since my family came from not too far from Pilsen. The classic Pilsener style is very distinctive with high malt content and high bitterness, which is why Michael Jackson noted that its firm malt body was almost southern despite its northern Germany origin. The German Beck's is also very close in style (about 3.5 percent apparent extract and 30 IBUs). In northern Germany, there are different styles that are drier and more bitter tasting, including the Dortmund style (at about 25 to 30 IBUs but 2.5 to 3.0 percent apparent extract) — a beer with less malt body, but about the same amount of hops.

In analyzing bitterness and body, you can see the difference in American and European tastes in beer. The European tastes run from Carlsberg (less apparent extract than Bud or Miller, but about 20 IBUs) to Pilsner Urquell. American tastes run from Miller Light to Corona and the American Lowenbrau — much lower bitterness and only somewhat malt taste.

Of course, Guinness Extra Stout is off the chart, with its IBU of over 50. The only way it can carry that level of bitterness is with a lot of black malt, which gives a sweetness that is not visible when you're only analyzing apparent extract. That is why it appears in a funny place on my chart.

Let's have a few questions before we study the beers.

Q: How does water fit into beer formulation?

JK: As long as water is clean, pure, and with the right mineral content, it isn't a major factor. Budweiser, for instance, makes the same beer from Tampa, Florida water, as it does from water from the Mississippi or the Merrimack rivers, or even from Newark water. Water is most important in your advertising, less important in brewing.

Q: Would you define apparent extract?

JK: The apparent extract is the amount of extract in the beer (i.e., the real extract) modified by the amount of alcohol. The more dextrins and sugars in the beer, the higher the apparent extract: the higher the alcohol, the lower the apparent extract. It is a result of those two factors, and can be measured with a saccharometer.

Tasting for Flavor Components

Let's try the beers. The purpose of this tasting is to give you really light beers with specific flavor components added or removed for you to identify.

Of these, the first is the flagship brand of one of the big five American brewers. It is one of the few remaining major beers in the United States that still has a noticeable amount of sulfur in the nose. Years ago, a sulfur nose was very common in beer. When my dad was a brewmaster, it was almost a desired characteristic, especially in the Midwest. Now, the sulfur nose has mostly been bred out of beer by changing yeasts. The second in the first set is the same beer with a couple of drops of copper sulfate solution, which ties up and reduces the sulfur. Can you smell the difference? Smell this only; please don't drink it.

The next set will consist of Budweiser with diacetyl artificially added to it. The second in that set is Budweiser with the diacetyl added, and also hydroxylamine hydrochloride, which reduces diacetyl. Again, only smell the sample.

The third set is an experimental brew which was taken to completion. Its purpose was to try to pull simple amino acids into the flavor. This was done by controlling the mashing and fermentation to get malt flavors. There are a lot of grainy, husky malt flavors that can be pulled into the forefront of the beer by manipulating the mash and the fermentation. The second in that pair has had alcohol added, which eliminates the graininess of malt flavor. This is a little known role of alcohol. I have never seen it mentioned in the literature, but you can clearly taste the way the alcohol masks the grainy flavors.

The fourth pair is fresh beer and old beer, using Samuel Adams as an example. The first Samuel Adams is one month old, and the second is over four months old. When beer gets old, it tastes more bitter, but objectively (and measured in IBUs), the bitterness stays the same. If you can isolate bitterness from sourness, which standards allow you do to, you can see the change. When beer oxidizes, the primary taste is the sourness, not the bitterness.

Pair No.1

Pour about two ounces of the first two beers into two cups. Just smell these: don't taste them. "A" is undoctored beer, which has a sulfury taste, that to me, is a murky flavor. It is probably the result of mercaptan, which is produced by the natural metabolism of the brewery's yeast. Thirty years ago, beer drinkers would probably have preferred this one. Even today, it seems to me that Midwest drinkers still prefer a sulfury taste, as do Australians.

"B" is the same beer with the sulfur chemically removed by copper sulfate, and it seems to me to smell fresher.

Pair No. 2

Of the next set, "C" is Budweiser to which diacetyl has been added at about 10 parts per million. I have been told that about 20 percent of the population is smell-blind to diacetyl. "D" is Budweiser with diacetyl, and also with six or so drops of a hydroxylamine hydrochloride solution that changes the diacetyl into a nonaromatic form. In "D" you can smell the Bud, not the diacetyl. In brewing, diacetyl can be eliminated by kraeusening and longer aging; the additional action of the yeast decreases the diacetyl.

Pair No. 3

In the next set of beers, "E" is beer that, through changing mash temperatures, overpitching the yeast, and underaerating the wort, has more malt flavors. These occur in the form of simple amino acids and give the beer a full taste unusual in an American beer because Americans seem to dislike the taste of malt in the forefront of the flavor. In "E" you can smell the malt aroma, and in "F" that smell is greatly reduced. Yet "F" is the same as "E" except that it has more alcohol: 6 percent compared to 4 percent in "E." This alcohol, which came from a bottle of vodka, helps mask the malty flavor.

Pair No. 4

"G" and "H" are identical, except that "G" is a one-month-old Samuel Adams and "H" is a four-and-a-half-month-old Samuel Adams. Most Americans are not familiar with the concept of drinking beer fresh — not that it matters as much with light beers. After all, what is the shelf-life of soda pop? Imported beers, for example, are often strongly oxidized. As a matter of fact, some people might prefer the older sample here, which seems to taste a little more bitter. Beer with a lot of flavor is noticeably unstable, and should be consumed while fresh. In older beer, much of the hop character is lost, with the bouquet going first.

The difference between "G" and "H" is in the sour taste. The bitterness is identical, even though old beer seems to taste more bitter. Samuel Adams runs slightly under "3" in bitterness, and in sourness, it is about "2" when it is fresh, and about "3" when it is four months old.

Q: Do you date your bottles?

JK: Yes, although as yet, no one in the U.S., myself included, has been willing to use a consumer-readable code. On the left-hand side of the Samuel Adams label is a series of notches that show the year, month and day of bottling. But you need a special code card, like the one I carry in my wallet at all times, to read the notches. By the end of the year, I am going to a consumer-readable code.

Of course, then some retailers won't want to carry the beer because they will get returns. But I think that a brewer's responsibility to give his customers great beer doesn't end when the beer leaves the brewery.

Jim Koch, president of Boston Beer Company, is a graduate of Harvard College, Law School and Business School. He returned to his family vocation of brewing upon the revival of traditional beers. Using an old family recipe, he created Samuel Adams Boston Lager, twice the first-place winner at the Great American Beer Festival popular poll. Jim's new brewery will be completed in early 1988, in Boston, Massachusetts.

Jeff Mendel studies entries in National Homebrew Competition.

2.
Contemporary Brewing Scene
A Growing Love Affair with Good Beer

Mark Carpenter
Anchor Brewing Company, San Francisco, Calif.

In taking a look at the title of my talk, "A Growing Love Affair with Good Beer," I feel as if I have been given the job of telling you what you already know. You are all involved in the contemporary brewing scene. It is true that there is currently a love affair with good beer, but it is an old love affair. For example, I have here an article from the *New York Times* entitled "Does civilization owe a debt to beer?" The author, Dr. Solomon Katz, contends that civilization may have started because of neolithic, nomadic tribes settling in one place long enough to make beer. So you see, our roots run deep.

The article reads:

"The event that primed the pump, according to the new hypothesis, was the accidental discovery by prehistoric humans that the wild wheat soaked in water to make gruel, if left out in the open air, did not spoil. Instead, natural yeast in the air converted it into a dark, bubbly brew. It made whoever drank it feel good. Also, (it) made people robust. At the time, it was second only to animal proteins as a nutritional source."

The author says that this fermented liquid made people feel good, and that is an important part of our business. We are in the beer business to make beer and to make money, but also to have a good time and make people feel good. Last night at the Great American Beer Festival, it was certainly evident that people were having fun; it was clear that the magic was working.

Mark Carpenter

The article goes on, "The world's oldest recipe written on Sumerian tablets is for beer." I think that is terrific! The tablets also held hymns to the beer goddess named Kasi, which is quite remarkable. From this, we see that the love of beer is an ancient tradition. In the history of the United States, the log of the Mayflower states that the pilgrims landed at Plymouth Rock rather than heading toward Virginia, their planned destination, because they were running out of supplies — especially beer.

The title of this year's conference, "The Year of the Beer," is right on target, in my opinion. This certainly is the year of the beer, and hopefully, it will extend for many years. Everywhere you look, the swing towards the popularity of beer seems to be genuine and pervasive. In any major city you visit, if you look down the bar, you see beer.

It used to be that if you wanted to see over twenty tap

handles in a bar, you had to go to Seattle. But I was just in a bar in Denver with over twenty tap handles, and there are many, many bars across the country with eight or ten tap handles of beers on draft. People are drinking beer!

In California, and in the West, Corona seems to have made it all right for mainstream women to stand up at the bar and drink beer out of a bottle. Rolling Rock seems to be having the same influence in the East. I don't mean this as a sexist comment, but it seems to me that while men were switching away from spirits to drinking beer, women still preferred white wines and light mixed drinks. Now women seem to be finding beer more drinkable, which is a good sign for us. How far this trend will go — and for how long — we won't know until it starts back the other way. But hopefully, it will last.

The one place the pendulum has not yet swung in our favor is getting people to drink beer with food. As small brewers, we don't have many advertising dollars, but we do have time. We need to spend the time to educate restaurateurs and the public.

In 1965, before Fritz Maytag bought the Anchor Brewing Company, he was sent to look at it by a good friend of his who wanted him to see it — not with the intention of buying it, but because it was a small brewery going out of business. Fritz' friend felt that the brewery had roots in the California Gold Rush, that it was the only steam beer brewery since 1919, and that Fritz might be interested in seeing it.

Fritz fell in love with it, bought it, and the first thing he wanted to do was to turn the product around to make it a quality product. In 1971, when I started with the brewery and it had just started bottling, the brewery sold about 600 barrels of beer. Then, there were only three of us working in the brewery. We had a fairly large brewhouse for a small brewery, since the facility had been a larger brewery that had fallen on hard times. We had a fifty-seven-barrel kettle, which meant that we didn't have to brew too often to produce 600 barrels. We would decide to make a brew on Tuesday, but if something came up, we would just put it off a few days.

So, the three of us would brew beer. Then we would move it to the cellar. Then we would rack it and bottle it. We would put it in the cold box and wait for it to sell. And while we waited for it to sell, we would paint the brewery. I can tell you that until 1974, there was an awfully lot of fresh paint around the brewery.

Then in 1974, a lot of things came together for us. The *New West Magazine* published a nice article about Anchor Brewing, and things really started to move. From 1971 to 1974, there were four breweries in San Francisco. In addition to Anchor Brewing, there was General Brewing's Lucky Lager Brewery, which is now just sitting around waiting for someone to revive it; the Hamm's Brewery, which is completely out of business now; and the Burgermeister Brewery, which was once the largest brewery west of the Mississippi and which is now out of business.

For awhile, we were the only brewery in San Francisco. During that time, we expanded, hired more people and made more beer. Now, again, there are two breweries, since this year, San Francisco Brewing Company has opened. It is a brewpub and a very nice place in a beautiful location. In fact, it is doing quite well in a downtown financial district, which I take as an incredible sign that mainstream Americans — business people — are drinking unusual beers and enjoying them. Two more brewpubs are planned to open soon in San Francisco, and the city will be back to having four breweries.

I remember a conversation I had with Fritz in 1973 when I was concerned about all the brewery closings in San Francisco. He said, "Listen Mark, in a short time you're going to see lots of small breweries opening everywhere." I wasn't too sure. Small retail brewers were having a hard time, and beer sales in general were down. But what Fritz predicted has come true.

Recently I was curious about where Fritz had gotten his insight on the future of the brewing industry. I recounted the conversation to him and asked him what had made him feel that way. His answer was, "Did I say that?"

But Fritz has certainly had a clear vision of where this industry was going and where he wanted to position Anchor Brewing. Small breweries in the United States have more than doubled in the last ten years and are opening at a very rapid pace. A person used to be able to keep up with them through the grapevine, but now it is hard to know them all.

One sign of the times is that major brewers are advertising dark beers, roasted malts and full-bodied flavor—flavor you can see. The most surprising to me was when Miller Brewing Company test marketed a wheat beer. It seemed incredible. Anchor Brewing Company came out with a wheat beer — the first in the U.S. — because we wanted a light, summertime beer for the few hot days in San Francisco. We didn't want to get into the lager competition, so we looked at other types of light, thirst-quenching types of beers, and wheat beer was the logical choice.

We tried to market our wheat beer as a summertime beer, but beer distributors are not interested in taking a beer available only in the summer. We have always had an easy time selling Christmas ales; distributors like them because Christmas is their slow time. But they don't want the wheat beer. If we decide to market it, which I believe we will, it will have to become a year-round product.

A wonderful sign of the success of beer is the number of existing microbreweries that are expanding. According to *Brewer's Digest*, all the the microbreweries put together produced 65,000 barrels of beer in 1986. But I think that is a false number. To that number, you have to add Anchor Brewing's beers and many of the contract brewers' beers, all of which the general public perceives in the same category. This would amount to well over 100,000 barrels of beer.

Do you have to be small to make a good beer? I don't necessarily believe so. The big brewers may very well come out with a beer as good as microbrewed beer. But I think it helps to be small. When you are a small brewer, you are paying attention to the product. At Anchor Brewing we brewed 41,777 barrels of beer in 1986, but we have designed our production so that we are still a one-shift, five-day-a-week operation. Any of our employees can go into any bar anywhere and see a bottle or glass of Anchor Steam beer and know they had a part in making that beer: it wasn't the night shift, it was them! They have an intimate involvement in the beer, which is very important for small brewers.

Just a little story: you all know how much care it takes to make beer on a small scale. You can't turn it over to someone else to do in a casual manner because it takes lots of attention. That is where the small brewer has the advantage. Well, one of our brewers decided to make some home beer. We have a lot of homebrewers visit the brewery, and he thought he would just whip up a batch so he could talk to them about the process. But he wound up dumping his first batch, and he came through the experience very humble and with a new respect for homebrewers.

Homebrewers and small and regional brewers especially, but all brewers are very proud of their products. There is a magic to brewing. Years ago, when there were only large breweries, brewery tours were very popular. People would sit around the tap room enjoying a beer, and the brewers I met at Hamm's, Falstaff and Burgermeister when Anchor was getting started were extremely helpful in giving us advice and tried very hard to brew the best beer they could. It is a tradition that is still alive and well today. Brewers want to serve their friends something they will enjoy.

Being small offers a few advantages, however, one being that a small brewer can take risks. If a holiday is coming or a special community event, he can produce a commemorative brew for it, where a large brewery would miss it by a year. And a small brewer can do unusual things with his beer. Even if no one likes it, it is only a small amount, and next year he can change it.

By the way, Anchor Brewing has always tried to be helpful to small brewers. If we can help you, feel free to call on us. I have often heard Fritz say that if we are ever the second smallest brewery in the United States, he would certainly be nicer to the first smallest brewery than many people were to us, although we did have many good friends.

I mentioned Corona and Rolling Rock a few minutes ago, and I must comment that I hate seeing beer drunk from the bottle. I have brought along a short demonstration about how beer should be drunk. First, you need a good beer; you will see here that I have some Anchor Steam beer. Next you need a Swiss army knife because most good beers come with a pry-off cap. Then, I advise you to get a glass big enough to hold the whole beer, plus the head. With a glass, you are releasing the carbonation and also the aroma. You have a chance to enjoy the entire beer: you can look at the color — the beauty of the head, you can smell it, and then you can taste it.

Mmmmmmmmmm, tastes good!

Mark Carpenter started working with the Anchor Brewing Company in San Francisco in 1971, when it was just a small brewery on Eighth Street, and he was as young as green beer. Having learned the brewing trade hands-on, he is now Anchor's production manager.

3.
Recipe Formulation
Improve Your Ability to Write Beer Recipes

Byron Burch
Great Fermentations, San Rafael, Calif.

The focus of this talk is recipe formulation or design, which means that I am supposed to share with you the rather esoteric, technical data I use in developing recipes for specific types of beers. I will probably address some of that, but what I am actually going to talk about is a hypothetical situation in which you make a beer style unfamiliar to you. I will indicate some of your concerns in approaching a new style for the first time.

Let's say, for example, that you have decided to make an all-grain amber lager in the Vienna/Marzen/Oktoberfest tradition, and that you have never before tried your hand at this particular style of brew. What do you do? Well, in whatever order you prefer, you would probably proceed as follows.

One of the first things, of course, is to surround yourself with a goodly number of beers representing the style, and set about conducting some exhaustive research. I must confess that I can never remember — and I suppose that it doesn't really matter -- whether this would be considered a "vertical" or "horizontal" tasting. In my experience, any worthwhile tasting begins vertically.

In any case, when you have finished, review your tasting notes on all of the beers. If you have tasted similar beers in the past, review those notes as well. Then it is time to go to the literature and analyze the problem from a technical standpoint, getting out all the books and magazines.

Byron Burch

Once you have thoroughly researched the style, there is only one place left to look: get out your *All-Grain Issue* of *zymurgy* (1985), turn to page seventy-three, read Gary Bauer's recipe for "Vienna," and do everything he tells you to do.

"Vienna"
Vienna-Style Lager

Ingredients for five gallons.
6 1/2 lbs. six-row malt, preground
2 lbs. Munich malt, preground
1/2 lb. Cara-Crystal (dextrine) malt, preground
1/2 oz. Hallertauer (10 percent) hop pellets (1 hour)
1/4 oz. Hallertauer hops (40 minutes)
1/4 oz. Hallertauer hops (15 minutes)
No. 308 (home cultured lager yeast
CO_2 pressure for carbonation.

Brewer's specifics.
Mash grains at 156 degrees F for 90 minutes.
Original specific gravity: 1.050
Terminal specific gravity: 1.012
Double-stage fermentation in glass at 38 degrees F for 4 weeks
Age when judged (since bottling): 3 1/2 weeks

Judge's comments.
"Great job on appearance. Beautiful aroma; a nice bit of butterlike diacetyl lends itself to malt. I suspect this is a ringer! Wonderful stuff, professional quality. A bit high in diacetyl, but class A+ brew." "Beautiful brew; a nice deep amber to light auburn color; decent head retention. Malty floral smoothness in the aroma — suggests richness. Lovely brew."
© *zymurgy* Magazine, Vol. 8 No. 4 ,
Used by permission from the publisher.

My somewhat facetious point is that basically, just about everything you need to know to make a very respectable grain beer in many of the more popular styles is already in the homebrewing literature. To get the information you need, you may have to look in only one or two places. In a sense, then, this may be an exercise in the mundane, but I hope not completely so. Certainly Gary Bauer is one of the most accessible sources of information for advanced homebrewers today. If you were looking into this style of beer for the first time, you could do a lot worse than to follow his suggestions. If you were making a different style, perhaps you initially could follow someone else's recipe. Normally, I would start by reviewing the

"Winner's Circle" recipes in my collection of the past several years of *zymurgy* magazines.

The next step is to analyze the recipe. Let's do that with the "Vienna" recipe above, touching on the following areas: malts and other fermentables, hops, yeasts, water, and techniques. I would like to start, however, with a general note on the subject of complexity.

If you have read, as you should have, Greg Noonan's article "What Makes a Champion Beer?" in *zymurgy*, Spring 1987, you will recall his emphasis on using several sources of fermentable extract in making most beers for reasons of complexity. He is right! I know some of you have heard my favorite "complexity" story, but it bears repeating because it makes the point so well. At a professional winemakers' conference in San Diego several years ago, someone offered a report on hydrogen sulfide (H_2S). H_2S is truly noxious stuff, detectable on the palate at five parts per billion and measurable by instruments down to levels of only two parts per billion. The study showed that wines having H_2S at the level of threshold detectability — but not so high that it could be recognized — were invariably judged more interesting than the same wine without any H_2S.

Obviously, this is the sort of story I hesitate to tell beginning brewers or winemakers, but it does make a point. No matter how noxious the element, if it is present at the exact level of palate detectability, it will add interest and not detract from the beer or wine.

If this point is worth making in terms of malts, it is ever more so with regard to hops. As Greg Noonan points out, if your Imperial Stout has seven extract sources and four varieties of hops, added at two different times during the boil to extract different acid complexes (not to mention two more varieties dry-hopped), competition judges may well be impressed by its complex intensity.

Now, having made that point (and we will be coming back to it later), please note that I have selected a recipe that does not particularly illustrate it in order to make another point: that is, rules do not necessarily apply in every situation. The "Vienna" recipe has only three sources of extract, only two of which have much effect on the beer's flavor — six-row lager (Pilsener) malt and Munich. The dextrine malt also adds a bit of full mouth feel and perhaps a touch of sweetness. What is the difference in this situation? Why break Greg's rule?

Greg's article goes on to show that the winning brews in several categories in the 1986 National Homebrew Competition establish complexity in similar ways. Notably absent from his list, however, are any of the lighter and more delicate lagers. In those beers, a clean, delicate balance is more to the point than is complexity. Within the world of beers, such beers as Pilseners and Viennas are models of civilized restraint. Therefore, in making Gary's "Vienna" recipe, we are being a bit conservative as to the number of malts used. Let us take a look, however, at the grains he uses to see how the combination fits the style.

The first thing is to make sure that the color is appropriate. In the *All-Grain Issue* of *zymurgy*, we find another article by Gary called "The Influences of Raw Materials on the Production of All-Grain Beers." If you cannot remember anything else that I say, please remember that every advanced homebrewer should memorize this entire article, charts and all. If you don't understand it, study it until you do.

Table 2
Beer Styles

LAGERS	OG	COLOR	B.U.	AROMA	BODY
Volbier	44-48	2.6-4.5	18-24	estery-malty	med.
U.S. Lager	40-46	2.0-3.0	15-19	estery	med.light
Lite beer	38-42	1.8-2.5	17-20	neutral	light
Pilsener	47-50	2.5-4.0	26-35	fine hop	med.
Dortmunder	50-55	3.3-5.0	18-26	flowery-malty	med.
Vienna	46-50	8.0-10.0	24-29	fruity	med.
Munich dark	52-58	14-20	18-24	malty	full
Marzen	54-58	9.0-14.0	18-28	malty	--
Oktoberfest	55-58	7.5-11.0	18-23	malty	full
Bock	58-65	18-25	24-28	-----	--
Doppelbock	65-74	22-30	23-30	malty	full
Porter	45-50	---	18-24	malty	med.full
Black beer	43-52	26-38	20-26	caramel	med.

ALES

	OG	COLOR	B.U.	AROMA	BODY
Light	31-40	2.5-4.0	8-10	fruity	med.light
Cream	40-46	2.0-3.5	15-18	fine hop	med.
Kolsch	42-47	2.5-4.0	7-12	grainy	med.light
Bitter	37-42	6-8	17-23	fine hop	med.light
Best bitter	42-47	9-13	15-21	malty	med.
India Pale Ale	44-50	4-7	21-27	dry hop	med.
Mild Ale	32-40	12-16	10-14	malty	med.light
Brown Ale	34-44	10-14	8-13	nutty	med.
Pale ale	46-52	7.0-9.0	24-29	fruity	med.
Alt	46-51	9.0-13.0	24-29	malty	med.
Scottish Brown	41-48	18-26	10-14	malty	med.
Old Ale	58-65	38-45	21-28	licorice	full
Porter	40-47	24-36	16-19	roasted	med.
Dry Stout	40-46	35-48	21-25	sour	med.
Sweet Stout	44-47	30-39	12-18	malty	full
RussianStout	65-80	18-30	29-40	vinous	full
Barley Wine	70-95	22-37	30-40	vinous	full
Weizen	46-51	2.5-4.0	13-17	estery	full

zymurgy Magazine, Spring 1985

Byron Burch

Malts

One of the things we find in Table 1 is a color rating of 8 to 10 for the Vienna style of beers. Turning to Table 2, we see a way of figuring out what that means. Column one gives a color (lovibond) rating for each malt grain based on one pound per gallon. Our recipe uses 6.5 pounds of Pilsener malt, so 6.5 times the color rating of 2.2 is 14.3, and that, divided by 5 (gallons) gives us 2.86.

Next turn to the dextrine malt and multiply 0.5 pounds times the color rating of 7, which gives 3.5; this, divided by 5 (gallons) is 0.7. If you add 0.7 to the 2.86 we got from the Pilsener malt, it gives a total of 3.56.

Then turn to the two pounds of Munich malt the recipe calls for. Here we find a range that depends on whether we have light or dark Munich. Let's assume light Munich, and take 2 (pounds) times 5.5 (color rating), which gives 11. Eleven divided by 5 (gallons) gives a total of 2.2. Adding that to the previous sum gives us 5.76 and leaves us short of the 8 to 10 we are looking for.

For this reason, let's take dark Munich malt and make the same calculations: 2 (pounds) times 13 (color rating) divided by 5 yields 5.2. If we add that to the 3.56 we got from the Pilsener and dextrine malts, we have a total of 8.76, right within the 8 to 10 range we are looking for. At this point, I think we can make a good guess what kind of Munich malt Gary was using. Even though he doesn't tell us in the recipe, he does tell us, in effect, in his article.

Table 2
Malt Usage

COLOR (1lb/gal)	ENZYME ACTVITIY	TYPE	PROPERTIES
2.2	high	Pilsener-6row	light maltiness
2.0	high	Lager-2row	light maltiness
2.2	high	Wheat	grainy,wheaty
3.0	high	Pale (Ale)	fuller maltiness
4.0	medium	Vienna	flavor, color aroma
4.2	medium	Mild Ale	dry,malty, color
5.5	medium	Lt. Munich	aroma,malty,color
13.0	medium	Dk. Munich	aroma, malty,color
7.0	none	Cara-Pils	body,palate full ness, neutral flavor
22.0	none	Caramel-20	color,flavor,fullness
43.0	none	Caramel-40	caramel flavor and above
55.0	none	Crystal-2row	similar to above aromatic, sweet
65.0	none	Caramel-60	strong, harsher European flavor
30.0	little	Amber	color, biscuit flavor
65.0	none	Brown	smoky flavor, color
400.0	none	Chocolate	dark roasted flavor
520.0	none	Black	burnt acidic flavor color

Example: 5 gallons mild ale at S.G. 1.037, color medium amber

pounds needed = 5 x 37 divided by 28 per gallon

$\qquad$ = 6.6 pounds

mild ales malt 95%   .95 x 6.6 = 6.3 lbs.

crystal malt 3%   .03 x 6.6 = 0.2 lbs.

chocolate malt 2%   .02 x 6.6 = 0.1 lbs.

$\qquad$ Total = 6.6 lbs.

USES
lagers, Pilseners, with adjuncts
all-malt beers, European lagers
10-30% Belgium light beers, 30-60% wheat beers
main British ale malt
Dortmunder, pale bock
mild and brown ale, dark ales
Munich lager, Vienna, festbier
5-20% golden & amber lagers, 25-50% Munich dark, bock
light ales & lagers, with adjuncts
　　3-15%, head retention-body
5-20%, light ales, lagers & bocks
3-20%, sweeter, maltier beers,
　　bock Marzen, porter, brown ales
5-30%, pale, mild & brown ales,
　　sweet stouts, porters, old ales
3-15%, alt, dark lagers, porter,
　　doppelbock
Scottish brown & dark ales, stout
2-15%, old & nut brown ales
2-10% bock, porter, stout, Oktoberfest, mild ale
Stout, porter, bock, color adjustment

Color:　　6.3 x 4.2　= 26.5
　　　　　0.2 x 55　　= 11.0
　　　　　0.1 x 400 = 40.0
　　　　　　　　　　= 77.5
　　　　77.5 ÷ 5 = 15.5 color

Now let's look at how to do a quick jury-rig. Let's say that you can get only light Munich malt, and have colorless dextrin-powder, as I do, rather than dextrine malt. As in Gary's recipe, we want to arrive at a lovibond rating of 8.76. Start by adding the totals for the two pounds of light Munich malt (2.2) and the totals for 6.5 pounds Pilsener malt (2.86) for a total of 5.06. Subtract that from 8.76 and you can see we need to make up 3.7 more points.

Let's make it up with good, old, garden-variety Crystal malt (Caramel 40 on the chart). So 43 (lovibond) divided by 5 (gallons) is 8.6. We need 3.7 points, so 3.7 divided by 8.6 gives us 0.43, which tells us that we need 0.43 pounds to give us 3.7 point in five gallons. Added to the Pilsener malt and the light Munich malt, it will bring us to exactly 8.76, the color level we were after. Not that this is based on an hour-and-a-half sugar rest in the mash. You don't want to go over that, and less time will yield less color

Table 3
Malt Color Figures

Type	Lbs.	Color	Gallons	Totals
Pilsener	6.5 x 2.2	= 14.3 ÷ 5	=	2.86
Dextrine	0.5 x 7.0	= 3.5 ÷ 5	=	.70
Light Munich	2.0 x 5.5	= 11.0 ÷ 5	=	2.20
			=	5.76
Dark Munich	2.0 x 13.0	= 26.0 ÷ 5	=	5.20
				3.56
				8.76

Table 4
Jury Rig

Pilsener	2.86
Light Munich	2.20
Dextrin Powder	0.00
	5.06
desired	8.76
have so far	5.06
needed	3.70

Caramel 40 color 43 ÷ 5 gals. = 8.6
Needed 3.7 ÷ 8.6 = 0.43 (lbs. needed) to get 3.7

I must mention that if you are doing a jury-rig like this while trying to stay within a particular style, there is another factor to consider — the original (starting) gravity of the wort. In this case, Table 1 tells us that a Vienna should have an O.G. between 46 and 50. This means that you may have to do some fine tuning to figure out how well your prospective brew does in terms of its gravity. The amount of finesse required and the number of adjustments you have to make will depend on the efficiency of your malt mill, as well as your mashing and sparging system.

Also permit me a word about dextrin powder. I feel it is a significant addition to the homebrewer's arsenal, but all such products are not alike. Some malto-dextrin has corn sugar in it, and may be up to 70 percent fermentable, thereby defeating your purpose in adding it. I like dextrin powder, and I have used it in any number of situations, even more often in extract beers. But I stick to the 100 percent stuff. If I want to add corn sugar, I will do it myself knowingly.

Hops

When you get to hops, things can get confusing. Looking back at Table 1, you will find a column labeled B.U., for Bittering Units. The listing for Vienna gives a B.U. rating of 24 to 29. If you have been using the "homebrew bittering unit" system used in most articles in *zymurgy* (H.B.U.), you probably realize that it is a different system. There are too many units for this type of beer, and it is true, for a rough calculation, that you can take these units and divide by three to get an approximation of the H.B.U.

Table 5
Hop Calculations

Hops	Oz.	Alpha %		7.25	Boil Factor		Totals
1st Add.	0.5	x 10	÷	7.25 x	29	=	20.01
2nd Add.	0.25	x 10	÷	7.25 x	12	=	4.08
3rd Add	0.25	x 10	÷	7.25 x	8	=	2.72
							26.81

There are some advantages to this system, however, which is that of the American Society of Brewing Chemists (A.S.B.C.). I am indebted to Gary Bauer, by the way, for writing a detailed explanation for me. This is essentially the system detailed in the advanced brewing section of my book, *Brewing Quality Beers*. Its main advantage over the H.B.U. system is that it takes boiling time into account as well as the strength of the hops. As we will see, the boiling time is of the utmost importance. It also makes it easier to talk to our friends who are commercial brewers.

My simplified version of this system starts by multiplying the ounces of hops per five gallons times the alpha acid percentage. The result is then divided by the arbitrary figure of 7.25. Multiplying that resulting figure by a factor based on the length of time the hops are boiled, yields the number of A.S.B.C. bittering units.

For example, in the "Vienna" recipe we are looking at, Gary indicates that he is working with Hallertauer hops with an alpha acid percentage of 10. He adds them in three stages. The first lot is one-half ounce, so we take 0.5 times 10 which equals 5. This 5 divided by 7.25 yields 0.69. These hops are boiled for an hour, so since the factor range is 28 to 30 for boiling times of 45 to 75 minutes, we multiply 0.69 times 29 and get 20.01.

The second lot is one-fourth ounce, so we take 0.25 times 10 and get 2.5. Divided by 7.25, that yield is 0.34. For boiling times of 15 to 40 minutes, the factor range is 8 to 12. The boiling time here is 40 minutes, so 0.34 times 12 is 4.08.

The last addition is also one-fourth ounce, and the boiling time is 15 minutes, so the calculations are all the same as the last one except that 0.34 is multiplied by 8 instead of 12, and that gives you 2.72. Then to get the B.U. rating of this beer, you simply add up all the answers: 20.01 plus 4.08 plus 2.72 gives A.S.B.C. B.U. rating of 26.81 — right in the middle of the 24 to 29 range we are looking for.

Let me note two things before I move on. First, there are at least three places in the homebrew literature where you can find bittering unit guidelines consistent with the A.S.B.C. system: Gary's *zymurgy* article (strongest on lagers); Fred Eckhardt's good article in *Amateur Brewer Number 12;* and my discussion in *Brewing Quality Beers*, where the boiling time factor is presented in some detail.

Second, you did notice, didn't you, that with only one hop variety, though added three different times, we violated the rule about complexity again?

Technique

Now that we are finished with malt and hops, I think this is a good place to sneak in a few words about technique, specifically mashing temperature, just in case some people here are new to advanced brewing. If you have read at all about all-grain brewing, you know that the higher the mash temperature, up to approximately 160 degrees F, the greater the dextrin content of the wort. Beers resulting from this sort of mash give a lot of "full mouthfeel" and a touch of sweetness. They don't attenuate as fully as they would if mashed at a lower temperature, and that means that they have a bit less alcohol unless the brewer compensates with more fermentables.

The Vienna style we are working with today is full and sweet. Note that even though a high mashing temperature of 156 degrees F is called for, dextrine malt also is added to create a very dextrinous wort. If you eliminated the dextrine malt, and mashed in between 140 and 145 degrees F, you would end up with a very different beer — even with otherwise identical ingredients.

The thoery is quite straightforward. Barley malt has two groups of starch converting enzymes. Those that convert starch completely to fermentable sugar are most active in the 130 to 135 degree F range. Those that convert it into dextrins, molecules too complex for yeast to readily convert to fermentable form, are most active in the 150 degree F range. The mash temperature you select will increase or decrease the relative activity of one of these enzyme complexes and affect the character of the final wort. This topic has been covered in numerous places in the homebrew literature. Another way, of course, in which recipe design is affected by technique is in that the efficiency of your grinding, mashing and sparging techniques will determine how much grain is needed to get a particular sugar (and therefore, alcohol) content. Depending on your equipment, you may need to make adjustments.

Yeast

When we get to the topic of yeast, we find an area that requires comparative analysis over a period of time to ascertain the best with a series of tests. Gary uses the yeast strain #308 for "Vienna." I have made similar recipes with others, however, and enjoyed the beers very much. Yeast strains are a particularly subjective topic. Not everyone will agree on the best yeast for a given beer.

To find the strains you prefer, I recommend dividing the wort in half and fermenting each half with different strains. Comparing the results after you have done this with a number of batches will help establish your own preferences. I have been doing this for awhile, and I find it highly educational. Incidentally, don't rule out lager yeast if you are doing an ale, or ale yeast if you are doing a lager. Fermentation temperatures and conditions should affect your choice more than the "appropriateness" of the yeast strain to the type of beer, which continues to be a somewhat overrated factor.

Brewing Water

The last area is that of brewing water, an area that a number of homebrewers are starting to pay attention to. This is a large subject, and I am going to cheat and say only that I am using Santa Rosa city water, which requires no adjustment for a brew in the Vienna/Oktoberfest/Marzenbier class. That means that I don't have to do anything to the water in this case.

If you really want to explore the topic of water, there is an excellent and extensive section on brewing water for lager beers in Greg Noonan's book, *Brewing Lager Beer*. There also is a very useful summary of what to do for different types of beers in the article by Gary Bauer to which I have referred throughout this talk.

In conclusion, we have hypothetically made Gary's beer with a lot of help from Gary himself (along with some others). As we expected, it is excellent. You know, though, I can't help thinking that maybe it could use just a touch more complexity. I have to wonder what the jury-rigged version would be like with less (or lighter) Munich malt, using a bit of Crystal malt to add color and a caramel touch. And, you know, next time, I bet a blend of Cascade, Tettnanger, Hallertauer, and Spalt hops just might be dynamic.

Byron Burch is co-owner of Great Fermentations in San Rafael, California, and the author of Brewing Quality Beer. A respected authority on homebrewing, he won the coveted Homebrewer of the Year Award in 1986.

Ike from New Jersey: Two Beers
and Everyone Sing

4.
Desirable and Undesirable Beer Flavors
What They Are and Where They Originate

Charlie Papazian
Association of Brewers, Boulder, Colo.

The subject of desirable and undesirable beer flavors is one that a person could talk about for hours. At our conferences over the years, both professional and amateur brewers have given some excellent presentations on this topic, for example, Rao Palamand from the Anheuser-Busch Flavor Center, Ted Konis from the Siebel Institute, and Dr. George Fix. I also have spoken on the subject of where desirable and undesirable flavors originate, so today, I will take a different approach to this subject.

In the past, I have looked objectively at flavors, that is: which specific flavors and components of beer we should know about and how we can detect them. This time I want to share with you some of my personal experiences of beer flavors, many that I have experienced during judging or evaluating beer. Today, I will discuss six different styles of beer — which flavors we look for in those styles, and which are commonly found in them. For example, because of the brewing process and ingredients used in making a barley wine, that style of beer has unique desirable flavors; it also is more likely to have undesirable

OFFICIAL AHA/HWBTA
HOMEBREW COMPETITION
SCORE SHEET

Entry Number_____

Round No. _____ Category _____ Style _____

Judged By: _____

	Maximum Score	

BOUQUET/AROMA (As appropriate for style)   10   _____
  Malt (5)
  Hops (5)
  Other Fermentation Characteristics

APPEARANCE (As appropriate for style)   10   _____
  Color (4)
  Clarity (3)
  Head Retention (3)

FLAVOR (As appropriate for style)   15   _____
  Malt (3)
  Hops (3)
  Balance (4)
  Conditioning (3)
  Aftertaste (2)

BODY (Full or thin as appropriate for category)   5   _____

DRINKABILITY AND OVERALL
IMPRESSION   10   _____

TOTAL (50 possible points): _____

Scoring Guide: Excellent 40-50, Very Good 30-39, Good 25-29, Drinkable 20-24, Problem ‹20

COMMENTS:

☐ Alcoholic   ☐ Astringent   ☐ Nutty
☐ Fruity/Estery   ☐ Sulfury   ☐ Salty
☐ Sour/Acidic   ☐ Husky/Grainy   ☐ Sweet
☐ Phenolic/Medicinal ☐ Metallic
☐ Diacetyl/Buttery   ☐ Light Struck (skunky)
☐ Oxidized/Stale (winey, cardboard, rotten pineapple)

Bottle Inspection_____

Aroma _____

Appearance _____

Flavor_____

Overall _____

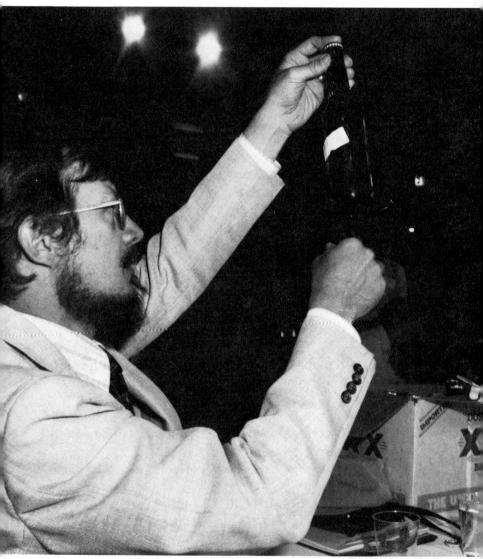

Gary Dolezal examines the bottle before he tastes the beer.

flavors that would probably not occur in brewing a stout or a Pilsener.

Before I start, however, I want to briefly list the objective flavors that are most readily apparent to homebrewers and beer evaluators. They appear on the score sheet used by the American Homebrewers Association and the Home Wine and Beer Trade Association in judging amateur brewing competitions. The list is by no means

Charlie Papazian

a complete list of all beer flavors as these are only about fifteen of the fifty or sixty flavors that a lab would list in evaluating beer flavors.

Fruity is a flavor and an aroma that we often try to detect.

Estery denotes the aromas and flavors that are applelike, raspberrylike, strawberrylike, and most often bananalike.

Solventlike is another character that I detect in homebrewed styles of beer with high alcohol and brewed at high temperatures.

Sour, or acidity, is a flavor often noticed by beer evaluators.

Phenolic is a character that I find is very difficult to identify and distinguish without training from someone who knows that flavor. Phenolic flavors range from the band-aid aroma (which may be a byproduct of fermentation) to medicinal, smoky and clovelike.

Diacetyl is a common butter or butterscotch flavor.

Musty is not as common as the others, but it is a moldy, musty flavor sometimes found in homebrews and corked import-styles of beers.

Astringent is a dry, puckery, bitter taste and sensation.

Sulfur denotes a whole range of flavors and aromas, for example, hydrogen sulfide (H_2S), a rotten-egg smell; sulfur dioxide (SO_2), a very pungent taste or aroma that can come from yeast or malt; lightstruck, a skunky taste resulting from a sulfur component; and dimethyl sulfide (DMS), a cornlike taste.

Metallic is a flavor that can come from the brewing pot or from the beer contacting aluminum pots, aluminum spoons, mild steel, or newly cleaned brewery pipes.

Salty is a beer flavor that was more prevalent in the past when brewers used packets of brewing salts to correct their water, not knowing what their real needs were.

Oxidized is a common flavor detectable in any kind of beer. Descriptors for this flavor are winy, sherrylike, cardboard or papery.

Winy or sherrylike is a typical oxidized flavor and aroma found in high-malt beers that are old.

These are the more common flavors and aromas that can occur in beer. Whether they are desirable or undesirable depends on the brewer's intentions. For example, metallic flavor or aroma are always very undesirable. Yet the sourness found in lambic beers is deliberate and a desirable flavor, while sourness is undesirable in home-brewed Pilsener. An important, desirable component of

barley wine is its fruity, esterlike character, and if it is
absent, the barley wine is not a classic, traditional English
barley wine.

Phenolic, a band-aid or medicinal flavor you might
think would always be undesirable, may be desirable in
very miniscule amounts to give certain beers a snappy
bite. Astringency, which may well come from the hard-
ness of the brewing water, gives certain styles of beer their
traditional taste.

As for mustiness, I have had beers such as Saison,
lambic and kriek beers that I have really enjoyed, but it
is my contention that corked beers such as these have a
musty flavor resulting from the cork. Or the musty flavor
could come from the wooden vats in which the beers are
brewed. In small amounts, this mustiness may define the
characteristics of certain beer styles. So you can see that
the judgment of whether a flavor is desirable or undesirable is relative to the style of the beer and the balance of
flavors.

Now I am going to discuss fruit beers, barley wines,
doppelbocks, Pilseners, Oktoberfests, Weizen, India Pale
Ale, and Imperial Stout. I had the pleasure of tasting six
categories of beers during first-round judging at the
National Homebrew Competition, and the beers, in general, showed phenomenal improvement in quality over
last year's entries. Still they had certain undesirable flavors that seemed indicative of the style. I would like to
address those now.

Fruit Beers

Of course, there is no one style of fruit beer. I believe

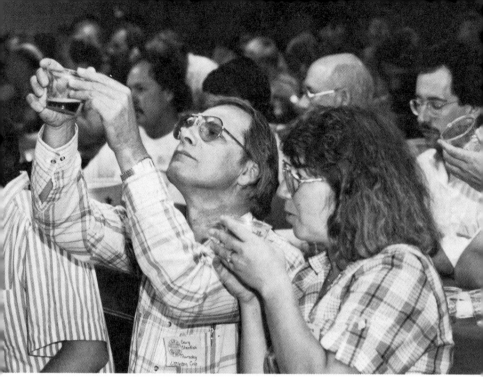

Learning to evaluate beers is part of their enjoyment.

that fruit beers should have not only a desirable balance of flavors, but also enough fruit to impart the flavor of the strawberries, cherries, or whatever was used. Sometimes, fruit beers are made with one pound of fruit for five gallons of beer, which gives the beer a blush of color, but no real fruit flavor. My thinking is that if beer is going to be evaluated as a fruit beer, it should have the character of the fruit.

You may wish to put three, four or eight pounds of fruit into a five-gallon batch of beer. This will give the beer fruit character, but if the beer is attenuated (meaning that it is dry with no residual sweetness), the fruit flavor still will not come through. Fruit beers should have a certain amount of malt sweetness, or sweetness, to complement and enhance the fruit flavor. Extremely dry fruit beers are out of balance, in my opinion, just as a too-dry wine would be out of balance.

To create a fruit beer that is high in alcohol but not overly sweet, you may wish to add honey, which ferments out. The drawback to putting a lot of malt into fruit beers is that it causes too much sweetness. But the honey boosts the alcohol of the fruit beer, without adding sweetness.

Undesirable flavors found in fruit beers are tannins and phenols. These are common in fruit beers because there are tannins in the skins and stems of the fruit. To avoid these, be careful not to let the beer sit too long on the fruit. If beer is lagered for weeks with the fruit, it will have a very astringent flavor that detracts from the fruity flavor.

Spicy, nonfruit flavors are also common in fruit beers. For example, you may brew an apple beer that tastes like bananas. This frequently results from the wild yeast found in the fruit. To avoid this, pasteurize the fruit. Do this by adding the fruit directly into the boiling wort and let it steep for fifteen to forty-five minutes. Don't bring the wort back up to a boil because the heat will set the pectin in the fruit and make the beer difficult to clarify. Wild yeast also can produce phenols, or medicinal flavors.

Fruit beers often take a long time to clarify. Keeping that in mind, if you are going to age a fruit beer, be careful not to allow the beer to contact air excessively. If you are not careful when siphoning the beer, oxidation will occur and will increase during the long aging time.

Further, fruit beers often have a strong diacetyl characteristic. Although I don't know exactly what causes this, I believe one remedy is to use a healthy yeast and wort that stays in suspension long enough to reduce the diacetyl. Using weak yeast in a fruit beer might result in strongly diacetyl beer.

Barley Wine

Simply put, barley wine is a style of beer that is very alcoholic and has a lot of malt and hops. Of course, there are other beers that have these same characteristics, but what makes barley wine distinctive is that it is brewed at warmer, ale temperatures. This produces alelike characteristics, particularly esters or fruity flavors.

In judging, I have found that barley wines are often not strong enough in alcohol flavor, and they are too sweet. Perhaps this is because the beer is out of balance, and the addition of hops may be able to reduce that sickly sweet flavor. But it is better to correct the sweetness at its source: the yeast. The sweetness is caused by the type of yeast that is being used, and its health. In making barley wine, it is important to use a yeast that can attenuate the wort very well. A weak yeast will result in partial fermentation and a beer that is not as alcoholic as it should be, and therefore too sweet.

Producing barley wine at colder temperatures should be avoided. First of all, barley wines are made with ale yeast to produce esters, and the esters cannot be produced as much at cooler temperatures. Also, ale yeasts are generally not healthy at cooler temperatures and drop out of fermentation too soon, resulting in a high diacetyl content. Yeast must remain in suspension long enough during fermentation to reduce the diacetyl. I have noticed this particular flaw in many of the barley wines I have judged.

Q: Can a strong lager yeast be used at lower temperatures to make barley wine?

CP: My opinion is that if you do this, you'll end up with a beer that is more like a doppelbock — lots of hops, lots of malt, lots of alcohol, but lacking the esters that are found in barley wines. And in judging, I have tasted some "barley wines" that were excellent doppelbocks.

Q: Does Champagne yeast produce the esters needed for barley wine?

CP: From what I have heard from winemakers, Champagne yeast gives a particular Champagne character. I don't believe that is what we are looking for in barley wine.

Back to my comments on making barley wine, when you are making a malt extract barley wine, you must be careful not to scorch the wort, which will result in the beer having a smoky flavor. Remember, the wort is so thick that it can easily be scorched, especially if it is being heated with an electric immersion heater or on an electric stove.

Also, choose a malt extract and design a mash with the maximum amount of fermentables. If you use a malt extract high in nonfermentables, you will get a beer with a high final gravity. Some malt extracts that attenuate well and ferment well are the German malt extracts, the dry English malt extracts, and the malt extracts designed for American Pilsener or light beer styles. If you use a highly fermentable malt, don't worry; you will still get plenty of sweetness in your barley wine.

Oxidation can be common in barley wine — as well as in doppelbock, because both beers are aged so long. It is therefore very, very important to be as careful as possible in transferring beer. Also, you must not leave much head space in the bottle. If you are brewing a special barley wine that you want to keep for five, ten or twenty years, you might wish to purge the top of the bottle with CO_2 to ensure that the beer won't become oxidized.

Doppelbock

I have touched on doppelbock in talking about barley wine. In a sense, doppelbock is the barley wine of the lager family. Now don't get me wrong about this! The main difference is that the yeast used in doppelbock are lager yeast; they ferment at cooler temperatures, and they don't produce as many estery flavors as do the ale yeast of barley wine. The lager yeast also don't produce as much diacetyl because they ferment at colder temperatures than ale yeast do, attenuate the wort, produce alcohol, stay in suspension for a longer period of time, and produce a characteristic lager flavor.

Doppelbock is sometimes as strong as barley wine and is therefore susceptible to being scorched in heating. Doppelbock can also have oxidation problems, as discussed above.

Pilsener

Because Pilsener is a light, delicate style of beer, it readily shows any flaws. Flavor deficiencies are easily detectable in Pilseners.

In making all-grain Pilseners, oversparging the grains can cause tannins and starches that can be the precursors for many other problems. One I have noticed is a grassy or cornlike flavor. Usually when I discuss this with the brewer, I ask how much he or she has sparged the grains. Often he or she will confide that the grains were sparged nearly forever to get everything possible out of them. This will definitely produce off-flavors in Pilseners.

Sparging too long can result in starches that produce a haze. The haze is flavorless, but it is then available to support certain types of bacteria that cause off-flavors and diacetyl.

Also, striking a careful balance of dextrins is important for aging Pilsener beers. In making a Pilsener, avoid extracts with a lot of dextrins. Some malt extracts that are good for Pilseners are those that attenuate very well: the German malt extracts, the Alexander Sun Country malt extracts from California, the dry malt extracts, and American Pilsener and light-beer beer kits. The John Bull plain light malt extracts are of very excellent quality and are very good for medium-to heavy-bodied beers, but they give high final gravity and should be avoided for making lighter-bodied Pilsener.

To make Pilsener, you must have a yeast that can behave in cooler temperatures without producing esters — a yeast that can ferment the beer to the degree desirable in the Pilsener style.

Water also is an important factor in making Pilsener beer because the beer-style is so light. I have detected chlorophenols in the Pilseners I have judged, and it is harsh bitterness resulting from water high in chlorine. If you really want to make a prize-winning Pilsener, pay attention to the chlorine content of the brewing water.

If you boil the wort too long in making Pilsener, the malt may become caramelized, and the beer will be a darker color than is desirable. The norm is, if you are boiling for two or three hours, you will begin to get a color that is inappropriate for your Pilsener.

Oktoberfest

One thing that contributes to the toasted, Vienna quality of Oktoberfest is toasting malt in the oven. This works fine, unless the malt is then oversparged, which results in tannins that give the beer an astringent, husky flavor. I noticed that flavor in many of the Oktoberfests in this year's competition. The beers had the great toasted flavor that could only come from home-toasted malt, but they also exhibited the puckery, tanninlike flavors that come from oversparging.

Weizen

Weizen beer should not be excessively bitter, but a number of Weizen beers in this year's competition were very overhopped. Wheat beers should have relatively low hop flavor.

As an aside, wheat malt extract has now become available, and someone recently asked me how much malted barley should be used with wheat malt extract. One of the main purposes for using malted barley in an all-grain wheat beer is that the husks from the malted barley serve as a filter bed. Wheat malt does not have husks to speak of, so a minimum of 30 percent malted barley in an all-grain mash provides a filter bed. Using the new wheat malt extracts, you can brew with 100 percent wheat.

Q: We have found that we get a smoky flavor, like that

in German Rauch beer, in using 100 percent wheat malt, and we use barley malt to balance that out.

CP: The typical style throughout the years is probably 30 percent malted barley because most brewers have not brewed with malt extract.

India Pale Ale

India Pale Ale is a floral, hoppy, bitter, alcoholic type of beer. IPA has a unique bitterness that comes from both hops and the brewing water, which in England has more mineral content.

If any of you are making IPA and want to duplicate the old tradition of using wood by adding oak chips, be careful how you use them. You can easily overdo it, and get a tremendous tannin character in your beer that is most unpleasant. The chips are generally added in the storage stage of the beer. Fermentation lasts three to five days traditionally, then instead of buying an expensive wooden barrel for storage, you add oak chips for twenty-four to forty-eight hours. This will add a significant character to the beer.

Imperial Stout

Imperial Stout is a style of beer that can be copper to black in color. It has a strong estery, fruity character, so bearing that in mind, use a yeast at an ale temperature to get that quality. If you try to make Imperial Stout at cold temperatures, you may get a great beer, but it won't be an Imperial Stout style.

The roasted barley and black malt give Imperial Stout

its characteristic copper or black color. I believe there is a roasted character in Imperial Stout, but it is not an astringent, harsh character that could be caused by adding too much roasted barley or black malt. Grant's Imperial Stout (brewed in Yakima, Washington) has a roasted, but not overbearing, quality.

Imperial Stout is well-aged, so oxidation can be a problem.

Charlie Papazian is president of the Association of Brewers in Boulder, Colorado, and is the publisher of zymurgy *and* The New Brewer. *He also is the author of* The Complete Joy of Home Brewing. *Charlie founded the American Homebrewers Association in 1978 and the Institute for Fermentation and Brewing Studies, an organization for commercial brewers, in 1983. Still, he regularly finds time to brew beer.*

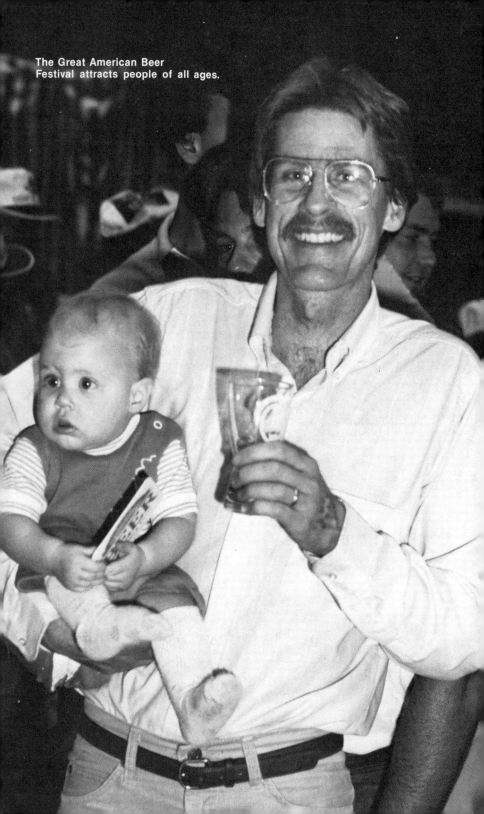

The Great American Beer
Festival attracts people of all ages.

5.
The Saxton Brewery
The World's Smallest Commercial Brewery

Dewayne Lee Saxton
The Saxton Brewery, Chico Calif.

This will be the best speech I have ever given, since it is the first speech I have ever given. I am president and master brewer at the Saxton Brewery in Chico, California, one of the smallest microbreweries in existence. We produce fifty-gallon batches, all by hand.

Chico — specifically the University at Chico — was recently rated by *Playboy Magazine* as the number one party college in the United States. Chico is nestled against the Sierra Nevada foothills on one side and the Sacramento River on the other. On any given weekend, you will find literally thousands of bodies floating down the Sacramento River on tubes, with kegs and stereo systems attached.

Chico has the second largest city park in the United States, extending from the Sacramento River up into the mountains. It is a nice place, except for one thing: I was always plagued by the saying, "If you don't want to work for minimum wage in Chico, there are 15,000 students who will." Needless to say, I had to find an occupation that I enjoyed and where I was my own boss.

Dewayne Lee Saxton

When I began homebrewing, my wife and I started a catering business. For twelve years, I was a chef specializing in soups and sauces. I had studied under James Beard, who said one thing I will never forget: "Everything you perceive is a spice, and you must blend spices to suit your own palate." I took that premise and applied it to water, yeast, malts, grains and hops, in creating my own brews.

I have done everything they say one can't do. I started brewing with malt extracts and dry malts, three different grains and five different hops, with never fewer than four hops in my brews. Now I am planning to open a pub, and I am trying to tame the brews down a little bit. Right now, I have no product under about 7.4 percent alcohol by volume, which I am trying to scale down to suit a pub atmosphere.

I originally began making an ale similar to Spaten. My first batch was good, and I was encouraged by friends to enter the Northern California Regional Homebrew Competition, and was fortunate enough to take first place in the light ale category. I was inspired by friends who had been to Germany and England to continue my brewing. They bought my materials, and I created a couple of new batches and entered the National Competition here in Denver, Colorado, where I took 1984 Homebrewer of the Year.

I was also brewing all the time while I was a chef, producing about eighty gallons a week to take care of my neighborhood friends. A friend with a bottle shop came up to me one day and said, "I get great reviews about your beer." So I started my brewery.

I immediately filed with the Bureau of Alcohol, Tobacco and Firearms to take care of the paperwork, and in doing so, I learned a lot about our so-called free enterprise system. We had so much paperwork to cope with that it took us almost two years to become legal. Then after we were finally legal, we had to submit label designs for approval. Finally, it took almost two-and-a-half years before we hit the retail shelves, which was two weeks before Christmas in 1985.

One thing we came across in completing the paperwork that would allow us to go from being a homebrewer to being a microbrewer was the sheer volume of paperwork. We just stepped back and gasped when we got it. One of the first forms required that we sign over our power of attorney to an attorney, so the government could deal with an attorney instead of us. But we found a way around that, although take my word for it, the attorneys didn't like it. My wife and I signed our power of attorney over to each other in front of an attorney, and thus kept the power over our brewery. Always remember that you will receive a lot of forms that are not required by law. Read and research every piece of paperwork you get from the federal, state and local government. Always look to see if the forms have number codes at the bottom that mean they are required.

Keep control over your situation. I am lucky enough to have a partner — my wife — who does all our label designs, poster designs, newsletters, and who also deals with the government. When the agents come around (I admit I have a little problem about wanting to inform our public servants that they are our servants), my wife sends me to the spring to get water. Then she takes over from there.

In a brewery, you also generate a lot of paperwork to keep track of things, so we created newsletters to send to our accounts. We were fortunate in that we never had to ask anyone to sell our ale. After we won the awards and used the press releases from the Association of Brewers to get publicity, we got immediate response from local, state and national brew magazines.

All the time we were starting our brewery, I kept in mind the law of compensation. The law of compensation states that what goes out, comes back — what goes around, comes around. I believe that what you put out, will come back to you tenfold, so you want to put out good. You want to speak well of everyone. For example, it is very important that all microbreweries support each other. In

California, we have many microbreweries and micropubs, and we together sponsor benefits and tastings all up and down the state. That way, we get publicity, and we get to know each other and work with each other. We all help set up accounts in different towns, and help spread the word about the "brotherhood of brew," my trademark and my song.

Personally, the law of compensation was very important to us. We didn't have any money when we started our brewery, and everyone told us it would take at least $150,000. Well, we do have a brewery, which we completely own without banks, backers or partners. It takes a little more time without financial backing, but you can do it alone.

Don't be afraid to research and design your own equipment. We didn't have much money, as I said, and I never took any shop classes in school, but I designed the equipment in about six months by asking people who know what they are talking about. I designed a 500-gallon stainless steel cookpot and an 860-gallon primary fermentation tank, which should be on-line in about three months (September 1987). The cookpot has a bottom raised four-inches, to which I have welded four stainless steel bolts to hold a steel heat plate two inches below the pot. This way there are 567,000 BTUs of heat underneath the cookpot, but without scorching. The way the air circulates under the pot, I get a nice, gentle, rolling boil just where I want it. I don't have to worry about wear and tear on the pot or off-flavors in the product.

It was tough going in the beginning, when we started the microbrewery. My wife and I both worked two jobs, twelve to eighteen hours a day. It was quite tiresome and took a lot of moral support between us. This would be true between any partners; it takes a lot of commitment and communication.

We do everything in the brewery by hand: cooking-down, racking, bottling, even hand-capping and hand-labeling our bottles. When the FDA came to inspect our plant, the agent was really surprised at the quality control we have over our hands-on product. We don't use any lubricants or bottling lines, fillers, etc., and we take the extra step to keep a sanitary and sterile environment. Especially when you are doing the process by hand, you have to do this. Little organisms can come from nowhere and cause a lot of problems. If you are brewing with your own money, you can't afford to have problems. You have to be on top of it.

Our spring water for brewing comes from an aquifer 4,700 feet up in the Sierras. People say that you can brew with water as long as it is filtered and pure, but we can taste that our water is special. Our water comes from a spring deep inside the earth. The force of the water being spiraled to the surface almost filters the water and deposits the minerals along the way. We have only thirty-six parts per million of trace minerals in the water.

At 4,700 feet, there is a little cave about 350 feet up the side of a hill. It is five feet long with a six-inch opening, where our brewing water flows out, never changing winter or summer. We run the water 350 feet down a line into fifty-five gallon drums that once held fruit juice.

Then, we use a deionizer conditioner, which puts a negative ion charge on the molecules of the water. This changes the atomic valence of the water, so that all of the water molecules are negatively charged and repellent.

This keeps the drums from getting scale-build up and deprives bacteria from getting a foothold. We drive the fifty-five-gallon drums to the brewery and siphon the water from them into five-gallon glass carboys. These are sealed to store our water cleanly.

Getting the water is sometimes a chore. The spring is fourteen miles off road, and to get there we have to drive seventy miles and through a creek. But still, it is nice to go into the mountains once a week for the water.

In keeping with the purity I am trying to achieve with my water and also with my life, my fermentation room and cook-down areas are illuminated with kiva lights, which are a full-spectrum lighting source. Germicidal bacterial lights — or UV lights — stop bacterial growth, but the kiva lights not only keep bacteria from growing, they also ionize the air and balance its pH. Kiva light is the pure spectrum of light similar to what you feel when you are sitting in the shade of a tree on a summer afternoon. That is why your food and beer taste better there. It is the proper lumes of light that your body needs to absorb to survive. I am not a microbiologist — I don't own a lab of any sort — and that is why we take the extra measure to keep purity in our product.

I brew with malt extract, although people shudder at the word "extract." California Concentrates knows what I want in purity, and so when they put extract in drums for me, they put a fifth of pure-grain alcohol on top instead of sulfurics or preservatives. Then when I get down to the bottom of the drum, I make a pretty good ten- or twenty-gallon homebrew batch.

I also use 100 percent dry malt imported from Australia in equal proportions. I was importing the malt extract from the brewery in Kumbauck, Germany, when I created my award-winning Du Bru Ale. But after Chernobyl, I decided to get closer to home; I didn't want people glowing in the dark from my brew.

I first used import hops from Germany and Australia, but now my hops all come from the Willamette Valley and the Yakima Region. We seem to get a lot better research here, and we are getting a lot better strains of hops. Also, it is nice to go up and walk through the hops and learn from the people who grow them. As I said, I mostly use five different kinds of hops in my brews, and never fewer than four.

There is a high alcohol percentage in my beer, but I like full-bodied brews. I like the heavier hop-malt ratio. But with the water and yeast strain I am using, I get a nice balance.

I have a six-and-a-half-hour cookdown process. That counts from the time I start heating the water until the time I have added the finishing hops after the fire has been off for an hour. My brews all have at least 20 percent wheat malt, and I use three grains, along with extract and dry malts. I use a lot of barley malt, and some roasted malt in our new products, Lion-Hearted Ale and Excaliber.

I have always stayed away from using Black Patent, until now. We have a new product I categorize as stout: it is dark, but you can see light through it; it is full-bodied, at 9 percent alcohol by weight; it has an excellent malt-hop balance ratio that creates a dry, crisp, roasted flavor at the end. It is called "Excaliber — The Stout with an Edge," and I am experimenting with using a little Black Patent in it for color.

A few last words about the microbrewery business. I

Dewayne Lee Saxton

would like to thank Fritz Maytag for his speech at the Master Brewers Association of the Americas for letting us know that we are "Micro-Calo" breweries. *Micro*, of course, means small; and *Calo* means fine. That is what we are going to start calling ourselves

Also, distribution is a stumbling block we didn't expect. At first, we took care of our own distribution, but now we are looking for distrubutors and have spoken with several throughout the U.S. who specialize in microbrewed beers. They have the knowledge and care to promote our beer, and I recommend that if you are looking for a distributor, look for one of those.

What is in the future for the Saxton Brewery? Even with the new tanks on line, we are still doing everything by hand. We employ two people besides my wife and myself, and we expect to produce 300 barrels this year, up from 80 last year.

Right now we are in the process of opening a brewpub in downtown Chico, in an historic three-story building built in 1909, with underground caverns and Chinese tunnels under the streets. We will have a brewery downstairs on one side, and a pub serving medieval cuisine on the other side. We will serve our own beers, made on premises, as well as Sierra Nevada Celebration Ale, St. Stan's, and a few others. We will promote our pub as a microbrewery market. There will be no Bud.

We are calling the operation the Colsax Castle. It is an interesting thing: Robin Hood was filmed in Chico in 1935 with Errol Flynn and Olivia deHaviland, hence our name and theme. When we started the brewery, we named the brews Ivanhoe Ale and the Lionhearted, and found that it all fit the theme of a castle. Now the castle has come along, and Excaliber and Battle Ax are being developed. Everything is seeming to fit.

We don't have money for advertising or promotionals besides tastings and benefits, so we have come out with our first poster, which we have printed in limited numbers. But instead of advertising our brewery so boldly, it is called "Tales of Chivalry" and talks about the brewing traditions of sovereignty and loyalty. It says:

"The Lion Big Heart offers an award-winning Saxton Ale to Ivanhoe, the perfect knight, and thus raises the stardard of chivalry forever. Accepted chivalrous virtues henceforth shall be bravery, sovereignty, loyalty, a lot of self-sacrifice, and the sharing of Saxton's live ale."

I would now like to sing a song for you that I wrote on the airplane on the way to the conference. To accompany me, my friend Dr. Ball (aka Detmar Straub) will juggle bottles and balls to enumerate the five great forces: earth, air, water, fire and fermentation.

> God bless this ale
> Du Bru Ale
> It's for sale.
>
> I was asked to come speak to you
> To fill you in on our fine brews
> We arrived here safe and sound
> To the world's largest party
> With brews all around
>
> So raise your glass in a toast
> To all of you brewing coast to coast

Here's to the brotherhood of the brew
Not just me, but all of you.

God bless this ale
Du Bru Ale
It's for sale.

(A tasting was held during Saxton's song, with everyone sampling Du Bru, Ivanhoe, Lionhearted, and Excaliber.)
Here's to our health, prosperity, and world peace. Cheers!

Dewayne Saxton is a homebrewer-turned-microbrewer. He took his skills pro after he won the 1984 Homebrewer of the Year award, and now successfully brews 300 gallons of beer a week in his Chico-based brewery. He is now selling limited partnerships in his new venture — Colsax Castle.

Dr. Ball (aka Detmar Straub) has a ball at the GABF.

6.

A Renaissance

The American Brewing Culture

Michael Jackson
London, England

We all have good days and bad days. I had a really bad day last week. It started well enough: I visited the Falstaff Brewery in Fort Wayne, Indiana, where Ballantine IPA is made. Ballantine IPA is still one of the most flavorful of the old, established, commercially brewed beers in this country, and the Falstaff is a very nice brewery.

After our visit to Falstaff, a friend from Chicago and I headed up towards Kalamazoo, Michigan, to the Kalamazoo Brewing Company, one of the newest and smallest breweries. But before we left, we thought we would hit the local bar for a quick drink. We went into a bar in Fort Wayne and asked for a Balantine's IPA. The bartender (who was wearing Bermuda shorts, which should have been a tip off to what followed) gave us a sheepish grin and said he didn't know what we were talking about.

I said, "Okay, I'll have a wild turkey." If they don't serve Ballantine in the town where it is produced, one wonders what hope there is.

We set off again towards Kalamazoo, not knowing that we were supposed to take the exit to Battle Creek. We

kept driving for many hours,
and by midnight, we were in
Lansing, Michigan. It was
rainy, and we were tired. We
checked into a fairly fancy
hotel and decided to have a
nightcap. The manager said,
"Sorry, sir. The bar closes at
midnight."

My friend demanded
proper service, and the reluc-
tant manager way-laid the
barman, who was just about
to go home. At this point, I
decided that I had better   Michael Jackson
shut up since my accent is noticeably English, and my
friend from Chicago walked up to the bar and said, "Two
Ballantine IPAs, please."

The barman just looked totally bemused. My friend
told him to never mind the IPA. "Then, we'll have Anchor
Steam," he said.

The barman looked him in the eye and asked, "What
country do you guys come from?"

My friend said, "Illinois." And we had another wild
turkey.

On bad days it seems that the beer renaissance has
hardly begun. Yet, on other days it seems that we are in
the midst of the biggest change in consumer tastes that
this country has ever seen. The first time I ever judged
homebrew in the United States, at this event six years ago,
I was stunned by the high quality. I still remember, all
these years later, tasting a pretty wonderful wheat beer.

Michael Jackson

Every year there are more stunning beers here. This year, they were all stunning, from the Dortmunder Export to the Belgium Saison to the barley wine. Six years ago it was hardly conceivable that we would be drinking beers like those in the United States; it was hardly conceivable that anyone in the homebrew movement would be trying to make beers like that. Today, I think it would stun and bewilder a lot of people in the commercial brewing industry to see those beers being made by homebrewers.

When I was here for the first time, the Boulder Brewing Company was the newest and one of the very few microbreweries in America. Now there are nearly sixty microbreweries. Whenever I have spoken here, I have always tried to put on my best Alastair Cooke manner and make a ripping, eloquent, inspirational speech describing this great beer renaissance. I have always taken great pains to try to summon up all the eloquence for which I am known, especially if there were national media present. The next day, if ever there was a peep of noise about this event in any of the newspapers, it always had a headline saying, "Suds, Buds, Belly Up To The Bar."

I sometimes wonder if the media will really ever understand what is going on. I speak with a foot in each camp because I am still a part of the media myself — sometimes being the interviewer, sometimes being the interviewee. I am not sure anyone understands what is going on.

I am not suggesting that we should stop trying to tell the media what is going on. But we all know that we shouldn't expect too much from them. The best we can do is to try, in all our diversity, to speak in a similar voice and make our message simple and direct in explaining that homebrewers are different from microbrewers; microbrewers are different from small, independent brewers; and that the specialty people in the big breweries are also different. But all of these four very distinct, very different groups of people are, in their own ways, parts of the same movement.

It is a movement, you know — despite bad days in Lansing, Michigan. It is a consumer-led movement. In the West, where it started, the movement seemed to take off almost like spontaneous combustion, which may be due, in part, to the existence of the wine industry in the West. In California, Washington, Oregon and British Columbia, people are accustomed to growing things that they drink. They are also accustomed to talking about them in a way that might seem self-serving. That is how the explosion happened in the West. If a brewer goes to his bank manager in the West and asks for funds to start a microbrewery, the banker knows the man is crazy, but he also knows that people once started boutique wineries that became successful. Getting money for microbrewing is much tougher in other parts of the country.

Despite the downers like what happened in Lansing, it is still hard for me to deal with the uppers in a bar in a place like Seattle — seeing people trying to decide which of the three unpasteurized, draft, top-fermented ales they are going to drink. The beers arrive in all their luscious coppery color in pint glasses, and then the drinkers discuss which has the most banana esters.

I have to pinch myself when I have that experience. I also have to pinch myself when I am in midwestern cities like Milwaukee and Chicago where the average blue-collar drinker still bellies up to the bar and orders a Miller

Lite, and someone standing beside him orders a dunkle-weizen. There are now ten or twelve wheat beers being produced in the United States, and it astonishes me to see people drinking a style of beer that has been extinct in this country since Prohibition.

In the Midwest, however, the background is a little more germaine to what we are experiencing. The big cities of the Midwest are unique markets: Chicago and Milwaukee are the only two places in the U.S. where beer tradition never really died — although almost. In those two places you have always been able to get imported wheat beers.

The big challenge is the East, the part of the country that imagines itself to be the most sophisticated and is, in fact, one of the most backward. But even in the East, things are beginning to change.

We must keep reminding Americans of their beer heritage. It is always exasperating and amusing when Americans say to me, "It must wonderful being a European. You have all that *history*."

I always remind them that America has tremendous history. American history excites me more than European history, partly because it is so much more recent. Big brewers sometimes tell me that they produce bland, light, gassy beers because people will drink more of them. The economic reality, these brewers tell me, is that they have to produce beers that people will drink. I remind them that for all their muscle and power and Madison Avenue influence, they are abysmal failures because the U.S. is twelfth in the world league of per capita drinkers.

Sometimes they then tell me that they would sell more beer if America had a brewing tradition. I then remind them that this country was founded by Germans,

Dutchmen, Irish and British who are still the dominant ethnic groups in this country. And they tell me the U.S. doesn't have brewing tradition.

In the East, in Boston, with what Jim Koch has done with Boston Brewing Company, people are very aware of beer. In New York, Manhattan Brewing Company and Old New York Brewing Company are doing a good business, but I don't think what they are doing has seeped through into the consciousness of the people of New York. It hasn't even seeped into the consciousness at the opinion-forming level, let alone the opinion receivers. It is on that opinion-forming level that we all must work.

Michael Jackson, from London England, is a tireless advocate of beer appreciation. He travels the world sampling beers in the name of research and championing the cause of good beer. His unique perspective has made dedicated listeners of his many fans. His books include World Guide to Beer *and the* Simon and Schuster Pocket Guide to Beer.

7.
American Brewing
One Hundred Years

Kihm Winship
Syracuse, New York

I'm going to talk about brewing history from 1870 to
1970 — not so much its names and dates, but how the
economy, technology, agriculture and sociology of the
United States have influenced the evolution of beer itself.
I became interested in the evolution of American beer
after I had my first mouthful of German beer. It was very
different from American beer, and yet our beers come from
British and German traditions.

My first question was, why did American beers have
to change? They didn't unless two things happened:
brewers don't have to innovate unless a competitor innovates, and the breweries don't have to change unless the
environment in which they are brewing changes. The
problem is that someone always innovates, and the environment always changes. Let's look at these two issues in
terms of concepts.

Ales vs. Lagers

A lot of histories talk about the lager revolution, or

how America was swept under by a wave of lager. That's not really true. Lager got off to a slow start. The first lager brewing in America was between 1840 and 1842, and the lager brewers at that time were also brewing ales. For the first forty years after lager was introduced, the ale breweries continued to grow. One book (*Beer, Its History and Its Economic Value as a National Beverage* by

Kihm Winship

Frederick Salem, Hartford, CT 1880; reprinted NY, ArnoPress, 1972), commenting on American brewing in 1880, said, "The brewing of ale advances so regularly from year to year as to offer no striking facts for comment."

Many people have the conception that lager came in, increased dramatically, and ale production decreased. But that is incorrect. For about forty years, ale continued to trend upward, and the lager brewers were going at a similar rate. In H.S. Corran's *A History of Brewing* (North Pomfret, VT, David and Charles, 1975), he cites the fact that, "In 1850, ale brewing on the British model was easily the commonest mode of production. Even by 1860 lager brewing accounted for less than a quarter of the annual (beer) production."

In 1870, according to *100 Years of Brewing* (The Western Brewers, 1903), "The large ale breweries outranked even the large lager beer breweries of New York

City, Albany and Boston. So for the first forty years, ale was still very popular, and ale breweries were still opening. If, in fact, the trend was away from ale, why would anyone open an ale brewery? Each style had its advantages, but lager evidently was a little easier to handle. The wastage of ale was about 15 percent, whereas wastage of lager was about 7.5 percent. So it was twice as likely that a keg of ale would explode on the way to the saloon.

Why did people drink ale? Again Salem's book, published in 1880, said:

"There is a large number who prefers the flavor of ale, others drink it from habit and will always do so, others drink it because they ape English fashions, others because of the comparatively secluded and unsocial character imported from England to our ale houses suits them better than the more social and gregarious customs of the lager beer gardens, some even because it is usually the more costly of the two beverages. Some doubtless prefer it because it usually contains a little more alcohol than lager beer, and very many use either beer indifferently according to circumstances and convenience."

I think that's a good catalogue of why people were still drinking ale forty years after the introduction of lager: flavor, habit, fashion, customs, cost, alcoholic content, and availability in the saloon. I think it's useful here to look at one ale brewery in particular, Lill and Diversey of Chicago. It started early, and by 1857 was the largest brewery in the western U.S. It survived the financial panic of that year and continued in the face of strong competition from the German lager beer brewers of Chicago. In 1869, one of the owners died, and in 1871, the great Chicago fire burnt the brewery to the ground. So this ale brewery closed not because people were tired of ale, but because the owners aged and died and the brewery was destroyed. Ale never went away, that's the important thing to remember.

New Technology

In the 1860s, 1870s, and especially in the 1880s, brewing technology changed dramatically, enabling brewers to change the beers they were brewing. New malting machines allowed them to do more uniform malting; steam heat allowed for precise control of boiling and mashing temperatures for the first time; and CO_2 injection, begun as a replacement for kraeusening, had the effect of limiting the amount of infection introduced into the beer. These factors allowed lagers to become more consistent.

Refrigeration did for fermentation what steam heat did for the mash and the boil: it allowed precise control. Louis Pasteur began his yeast studies in 1857, and by 1883 Carl Hansen had isolated a single-cell yeast culture. What these did was to give the brewers another measure of control.

Through technology, beers became more consistent. Pasteur's studies were published in 1876, but as early as 1872, the brewers knew about them, and Anheuser-Busch was pasteurizing its beers. This gave the national "shipping" brewers an advantage. Prior to this, only ale brewers had been able to ship bottled beer.

And lastly, texts and trade publications became available. In the 1880s, there were five different magazines for brewers, as well as major texts that provided brewing knowledge. As a result, the brewing trade became less reliant on father-son type of learning, and brewing knowledge became available to all brewers.

Barley vs. Corn

Why did brewers begin to use corn in beer? Let me quote the *United States Brewers Association Yearbook* from 1914: "Barley above all other grains is the most unpleasant to raise, harvest and thrash, and one of the most undesirable grains to market." The reason was that barley has little barbed awns that get stuck in a person's throat and clothes and that choke horses. Besides, barley doesn't yield as much per bushel as does corn. So there are problems in growing barley, which makes it more expensive than corn.

But there were other problems. When the German brewers came to America, they went from using a barley well-suited to all-malt beers to using a barley that had a much higher enzyme content. This caused a terrific protein haze in their beers.

There also was a problem with the supply and cost of barley when the government began putting tariffs on imported barley. Canadian barley was a superior product, but the government taxed its use in the U.S. to protect the local producers and improve American barley. The tariff made Canadian barley too expensive, and also pushed up the price of American barley. So the supply became limited and the cost of all barley increased.

About this time, the saloons began demanding

clearer, lighter, less expensive beers. According to Thomas Cochran's *The Pabst Brewing Company* (NY, NYU Press, 1948), John Pierce, Chicago manager for the Pabst Brewing Company, wrote to Fred Pabst in the spring of 1880 emphasizing the absolute necessity of lightness in color. In March 1880, he wrote, "Can't you give us a paler, purer beer?" I believe he is referring to a beer without chill or protein haze that makes the beer appear impure.

A few days later Pierce again wrote, "Our reputation in Chicago will certainly suffer if we don't get a different beer. Our customer Shaughnessy out on Graceland Road sent us word that he could not use our beer any longer, it being so dark."

So the brewers had another problem: they needed clearer, lighter beer.

Corn solves all these problems. It clears beer because its enzymes are used to convert the starch. It lightens the color of beer, and it is much cheaper. Essentially, the problems with barley are what drove brewers into the arms of the corn growers.

Pabst had started using small amounts of corn in 1870. By 1893, Pabst's standard beer was one part cornmeal to two parts malt. It is interesting that in spite of all this there were still some lovers of fine beers who preferred the old-style German products. According to Cochran, "these pure malt beers amounted to about one-tenth the total product brewed. The cost of materials for these brands, due to the larger percentage of malt and the use of more imported hops, ran as high as 80 to 100 percent more than the standard product. Yet the great majority of Americans preferred this latter, cheaper type."

Another bit of testimony, this time before a Senate committee that was investigating food adulteration in 1900, came from a New York City brewmaster who told the committee he used only malt in 75 percent of his beers. He also mentioned another beer made with corn grits. The chairman asked, "Do you have some customers who prefer that?"

The brewer replied, "I use it to meet competition. Some customers want a lighter beer because I can and do give it to them cheaper, the cost of production being less."

When people tell me that American beer has grown lighter because the public demands it, I don't believe them. These factors I have just mentioned have greatly influenced the lightening of beer.

There are also a number of other factors. For one, the technology for mass-producing glassware developed during the 1800s, and suddenly protein haze — which wasn't a problem in Germany where people were drinking out of mugs — became a problem when people could see it.

Also, the soft-drink industry started in 1835, and by 1879 there were 579 bottling plants in major cities all over America. These were in the same major cities that held 90 percent of the brewers market. So suddenly, after the eighteenth century, when the lightest drink was beer (cider or whiskey being more alcoholic), now in the nineteenth century there was something lighter than beer that gave the brewers competition.

When you think of it in terms of weights on a scale, all of these factors are weights that suddenly pressed brewers to make a lighter beer.

Industrialization

The need for sobriety was evident as America became more industrialized. In factories, machinery became more complex and less forgiving, and it became more hazardous for a person to be drunk at work. There is an old story about no matter how drunk a person was, the horse knew the way home. This changed when the automobile came into vogue.

Taxation

By lightening beers, brewers had a hope for a tax reduction. In 1914, the *United States Brewers Association Yearbook* said, "It must be remembered that in the European countries, where the sentiment for temperance is most advanced, direct encouragement is given to sales of light beers. In Scandinavian countries light beers are almost tax free."

The brewers also hoped that by lightening beer, they could evade Prohibition. The president of the USBA in 1896 said in a speech, "The percentage of alcohol in American beers is growing less from year to year. This fact ought to exempt our beer entirely from many of the restrictions now applied to intoxicants."

Economic Factors

There were also many economic reasons for brewers to start lightening their beers. First of all, anytime there was a crunch on the economy — and there were many between 1870 and 1919, brewers were forced to lighten up on ingredients. In price wars, smaller local brewers sold kegs of beer for eight dollars instead of nine, so wholesale prices went down. At the same time, labor costs went up because of unionization, which started about 1885. The first strikes and boycotts occurred in 1886, and all the Milwaukee brewers were boycotted. When management/union differences were resolved, labor costs went up.

The first excise tax during the Civil War was one dollar a barrel, which could not be passed along to the consumer. In the Spanish-American War of 1898, an additional dollar of excise tax was added. Government tariffs on barley and hops continued to rise. And still the saloons were demanding a lighter, cheaper product. Distribution costs for brewers who wanted to become national shippers, rose significantly as rail lines, refrigerator cars, ice stations along the routes, and branch offices had to be established. And everytime there was an advance in technology, if the brewer wanted to keep up and therefore stay in production, he had to buy new, expensive equipment.

At the same time, local Prohibition was starting to squeeze out the brewers. Michigan, for example, had statewide Prohibition two years before national Prohibition. All of these factors put the brewers between a rock and a hard place. The only thing that could give was what went into the beer.

Prohibition

Prohibition obviously had a huge effect on the brewing industry. The first thing we need to understand about Prohibition was that one of the main forces behind it were the saloons and the brewers. The brewers owned about 80 percent of the saloons in America. In the era before advertising, the only way a brewer could guarantee his share of the market was to own the saloon and insist that it sell only his beers.

Saloons had their positive side; they gave immigrant workers and lower classes a place where they were accepted — something they couldn't get from middle-class churches and clubs. The problem was that the brewers really capitalized on that. Four-fifths of saloon-keepers' business was beer, and to compete, the saloons were forced to stay open on Sundays and after hours. The negative side was that saloons became terribly corrupt institutions that fed on the battered self-esteem of the worker. Workers lived in poor tenements, but in the saloon, they were in an environment of cut glass, mirrors, shiny brass rails, and trophy heads hanging on the wall next to paintings of reclining, nude women. The image was that of "man the conqueror," which boosted their self-esteem.

The brewing companies invested tremendous amounts of money in these establishments. In 1887 to 1900, Pabst invested over $2 million in saloons, and Schlitz did the same thing. In Milwaukee, by 1898, Pabst had 250 saloons, and by 1907, it had nearly 400. In New York, George Ehret's Hellgate Brewery owned between 800 and 1,000 saloons.

The states tried to regulate the saloons by charging high license fees, but this worked exactly opposite the desired effect. The state charged saloon-keepers between $500 and $1,000 per year to stay open. Small saloons couldn't afford that fee, and hence they sold out to brewers.

Women didn't fare very well because of the saloon. Their husbands' pay envelopes were emptied by the saloons. One out of every three saloons was connected to a brothel, and the spread of venereal disease was phenomenal. The wives contracted the diseases, and the drunk husbands beat the kids. You can see why Prohibition was enacted so quickly.

Alcohol and beer also were a threat to industry. Workers would drink during lunch, and industrial accidents and absentism cut into productivity. The more industrialized America became, the more sensitive the capitalists became to the role of alcohol in business.

The anti-German sentiment in World War I was really what kicked Prohibition over the hump. In 1918, John Strange, a dry leader, said, "We have German enemies across the water, we have German enemies in this country, too. And the worst of all our German enemies, the most treacherous, the most menacing, are Pabst, Schlitz, Blatz and Miller. They are the worst Germans who inflicted themselves on a long-suffering people."

Breweries didn't help their own case. August Busch and his mother bought German war bonds. In the 1914 *Yearbook*, one of the speakers said, "Our hearts throb and our minds march in time in sympathy with the brave fellows who are in the ranks. And the members of the brewing industry have responded generously to the appeals that have been made for the wounded of all nations." The best the brewers could do was to give to all nations.

One historian said that Prohibitionists were never brushed by the spirit of tolerance, which seems a true enough statement. They would resort to all kinds of exaggerations and distortions — anything to bring about Prohibition. The brewers gave them a lot to work with. Of course, the Prohibitionists succeeded.

Beer Production During Prohibition

One thing American beer had during Prohibition was variety. You always read that the brewers made ice cream, malted milk and furniture to stay alive during Prohibition, but a lot of them made beer. They acquired permits to operate cereal beverage plants, and there were 500 cereal beverage plants by 1923 during Prohibition. Probably three of them could have supplied the cereal beverage demand in America.

During Prohibition breweries would often be dismantled by the federal authorities, which meant they would saw out a section of pipe. The brewers, of course, would take a section of rubber hose and hook it back up. When Marine Corps General Smedley D. Butler was sent to clean up Philadelphia, he found thirteen "dismantled" breweries running full blast. He was told that nothing could be done about it, and when he threatened to go to the police, he was notified by the U.S. Marshall's Office that any policeman entering a Philadelphia brewery would be shot. Nevertheless, he brought the thirteen brewers into city court. Charges against twelve were dismissed immediately, and the thirteenth paid a small fine.

In New York City, the Phoenix Brewery ostensibly produced breakfast cereal. Time and again the federal authorities tried to arrange a surprise raid, but they were thwarted by the city police who arrested the federal agents as they stood on the sidewalks, on the grounds that they were suspicious-looking characters. The Phoenix turned out 800,000 half barrels of beer per year, at the cost of $2.75 each. The barrels were marked up to $12 to distributors, and to $18 for saloon-keepers. The Phoenix netted $7.4 million per year.

In 1926, Prohibitionists reported to Congress that the number of brewery sites was 991: breweries operating with permits totaled 410; and breweries suspected of operating without permits totaled 581. This adds up to 991. A Prohibition agent in Albany, New York, reported that he was having trouble with the breweries in his district. Out of nine, two were honest, and the others had to be watched all the time, but he didn't have enough men.

Brewers needed a little muscle to operate illegally, and they turned to the mob for protection. Eventually, however, the muscle muscled them out of business. After 1925, most of the open breweries in the United States ran under mob control. Al Capone grossed $3.5 million a week just from the breweries in Chicago.

Of course, there was also homebrew. The Department of Agriculture had published pamphlets on how to make alcohol, and in true bureaucratic fashion, it continued to distribute these pamphlets long after the Eighteenth Amendment banned the manufacture and sale of alcoholic beverages.

World War I had created a sugar shortage and the Department of Agriculture recommended the use of malt syrup as a sugar substitute. Furthermore, they said, "Let's recommend that we put two and a half pound packages (of malt syrup) for sale in grocery stores to encourage people to use it." People did use it, which resulted in one part of the government trying to dry the country up and the other part helping to keep it wet. The annual average production of homebrew from 1920 to 1929 was eighty-three million gallons per year.

Before Prohibition there were only three malt plants operating in the United States. In 1929, there were 135. According to one story, a 1920s police raid in New Orleans on a distributor of malt syrups, hops and homebrew apparatus led to the capture of the names and addresses of 10,000 homebrewers.

H.L. Mencken, an editor and writer, commented, "This homebrew, when drinkable at all, was striking proof of the indomitable spirit of man."

Mencken made homebrew, and once complained about his yeasts. His friend Phil Goodman went to the Lowenbrau Brewery in Munich and brought back enough yeast for both he and Mencken.

But my favorite quote about homebrew comes from British author G.K. Chesterton, who was touring America during Prohibition. He wrote:

"The private brews differ very widely. Multitudes are quite harmless, and some are quite excellent. I know an American university where practically every one of the professors brews his own beer. Some are experimenting in two or three different kinds. But what is especially delightful is that with this widespread revival of the old human habit of homebrewing, much of the old human atmosphere that went with it has really reappeared."

Alley beer was produced by people who were successful with homebrew and decided to go commercial. They brewed large quantities, which were usually quite awful.

Kihm Winship

It was said by Prohibition Commissioner Roy Haynes that you can't keep liquor from dripping through a dotted line, and the border of Canada was no exception. One of my favorite statistics is this: Canadian wartime Prohibition expired on January 1, 1920, and on January 2, 1920, there was a sudden increase in demand for motorboat licenses. What does that tell you?

There were twenty-nine breweries in Ontario, and a comparable number in Quebec. In Michigan, for example, every week, 400,000 bottles of Canadian beer were smuggled across the Detroit River. In northern New York, kids would smuggle beer through the woods and over the border on their backs until they had enough money to buy a horse. People smuggled beer by car and in their boats. In northern New York, the most active bootlegger owned a forty-foot boat that was painted black and used at night. Fully loaded, it carried 400 cases of beer and was barely out of the water. People kept building on these successes, but one barge loaded with 93,960 bottles of ale, concealed under a load of hay, was captured.

Bootleggers were supplied at the border by special distributors set up by the cooperative Canadians. One such plant received thirty-five freight cars a week loaded with beer — 900 cases per car. A *New York Times* correspondent estimated that in 1925, 10 million gallons of beer were shipped into the U.S. from Quebec alone. In 1923, it was estimated that 800 cases of beer were delivered daily to Detroit in mislabeled freight cars.

Bootleggers even used to pull beer across the bottom of the Detroit River on sleds. When the river froze over in 1925, 1926 and 1930, bootleggers drove over the ice. One morning in 1930, a reporter from the *Detroit News*

counted seventy-five autos leaving the Canadian beer
docks and driving into the U.S.

Federal agents complained that when they pursued
the bootleggers on foot, and were able to shoot out the
bootleggers' tires, the bootleggers hopped out of their cars
and skated away. So the war of beer was won by imagination.

In 1928 at the peak of this beer traffic, America drank
more than half of the alcoholic beverages made in Canada.
It amounted to 3.5 million Imperial gallons of beer. Hence,
the slogan, "Drink Canada dry."

The editor of a German newspaper in Detroit stock-
piled a substantial amount of beer. The authorities raided
him and confiscated 6,000 bottles. Six months later, the
courts ruled that the raid was outside the law and ordered
his beer returned. Unfortunately, 700 bottles were miss-
ing.

H.L. Mencken had a terrific source for beer. He
worked in New York City during the week, and spent his
evenings in Union Hill, New Jersey, where there was
always plenty of beer. German ships were docking nearby
at the North River dock. One evening, with friend Phil
Goodman, he met a ship's orchestra in a speakeasy and
was invited to the ship for German Pilsner.

Mencken wrote:

"Thereafter we visited that lovely ship every
time it was in port, which was about once every
five weeks. Then, in a little while, we began to
add other ships from the same and allied lines. In
the end, we had a whole fleet of them and had
access to Pilsner three weeks out of four — and
not only Pilsner, but also Munchner, Dortmun-

der, Wurzburger, and Kulmbacher. It was a long
hoof down the dark pier, and a long climb from
the waterline up to H-deck. But we were both
under medical advice to take more exercise."

National Brands: Before and After Prohibition

To address again for a moment the factors that caused
beer to become more uniform, we must consider the part
that national distribution played. The national shippers
first began shipping lager about 1853 from Milwaukee to
Chicago. Milwaukee had a tremendous supply of natural
ice, which was helpful to shipping. Of course, bottling was
also a tremendous advantage to brewers, as were rail-
roads with branch offices. National shippers literally
covered the U.S.

National shippers used new technology to become
bigger. The first consolidation was in 1870 when Pabst
bought a neighboring brewery. Only local competition
kept the growth of the national shippers in check. Local
brewers owned a lot of saloons, making it difficult for
Pabst or Anheuser-Busch to enter a new market. But local
brewers lost their advantage after Prohibition because of
the death of saloons.

Trucks and hard roads also helped the national distributors grow. With these, distributors could quickly
ship beer to towns fifty miles away without a railroad.

Higher taxes made it much tougher on the smaller
brewers than on the larger ones.

The advent of packaged beer offered national shippers who could afford a new bottling or canning line a
tremendous advantage. Cans meant that beer could be

shipped more economically, since cans take only half the space of bottles. Also, packaged beer moved into the home. The home became a more attractive place to drink because of radio. Suddenly, people didn't have to talk to the other people in the house, they could turn on the radio.

World War II was the crunch, however. War is always a terrible thing for beer. Taxes increased immediately; there were shortages of grain, and then the grain was rationed. But the demand for beer increased dramatically. In spite of rationing and shortages, beer sales went from 53 million barrels in 1940 to 64 million barrels in 1942, 72 million barrels in 1943, 79 million barrels in 1944, and 81 million barrels in 1945. This demand, combined with ingredients shortages, meant that beer had to get lighter.

Edwin Anderson, president of the Detroit's Groebel Brewery Company, warned, "Already inferior beer has hurt our industry. Too many brewers, lured by big public demand for beer resulting from boom-time buying power, have let brewing standards go by the board in the mad race for volume. Beer cannot be watered indefinitely without the public catching on." (We still don't know if he was right.)

The final blow came from the post-war boom. More people had buying power, and bought the watered beer. Supermarkets made packaged beers more popular. Television did what radio once did.

In 1970 Phillip Morris acquired Miller Brewing, which two years later acquired the Meisterbrau Brands, including Lite, and we faced another lightening of American beers. Light beer, the way it is now marketed, is aimed at people over age 34, so older people will drink beer, and the brewers will have a larger audience.

I would like you to consider these factors when you hear it said that American beer has changed because of popular taste. I don't buy it. All these factors together are the reason why American beer is lighter.

Kihm Winship received his M.S.L.S. in library science from Syracuse University, before he became an advertising copywriter and won the coveted Clio Award for his role in the packaging of F.X. Matt Saranac 1888. He has written numerous beer articles and is writing a book on the evolution of beer in America.

"Cheers!" is the password of the night at the GABF.

8.
Home Filtration and Carbonation
Their Advantages and Techniques

Todd Hanson,
Sheboygan, Wisconsin

I would like to begin today by taking a moment to thank the people who got me into homebrewing and to reflect on how quickly we have progressed in this country from having almost nothing for homebrewers to having the most literate and well-supplied beer fanatics in the world.

In 1973 I lived through the start of the Watergate scandal via the BBC and the *London Times*. I was in London on a University of Wisconsin at Stevens Point semester abroad program. The university contracted with a young Englishman to suggest activities and plan outings for the forty students in the group. He mentioned that in past semesters a couple of the students had played a little rugby at a local club. A friend and I decided to give it a try, and that turned out to be the most rewarding experience of the entire trip. We played rugger Saturday afternoons and drank Whitbreads at the club Saturday nights. All was well with the world.

Knowing how much I had raved about English beer, one of the older fellows brought a bottle of homebrewed

beer to the club right before I
left. I was astounded that
people could homebrew good
beer. He gave me his recipe,
and I made my first batch of
beer back home in Wisconsin
that winter. Do you know the
only place I could find malt
extract and hops? In the old
Herter's sporting goods catalogue. You might remember
that catalogue. It was a
pleasure to read because
George Herter was an expert
on everything. Old George

Todd Hanson

must have made a little home brewski, too, because there
in the back of the catalogue — hidden among the Canadian
blueberry preserves and the smoked salmon — were a
couple of very discretely worded descriptions for malt
extract and hops.

I got my supplies, followed the hand-scratched recipe,
and soon sat back with a glass of the most beautiful,
golden, foamy, alcoholic crap I had ever tasted in my life!
But it got me hooked, and I have been brewing ever since.

I thought of all that again as I was preparing this
address because of how much it contrasts with the homebrewing scene today. Just take one thing — hops. We have
gone from a four-ounce brick of dried-up who-knows-what
to a dozen varieties. Each are not only alpha and beta
analyzed, but we have information on each variety's typical contents of oil, humulene, humulone, cohumulone,
etc., etc. They are packaged in oxygen-resistant bags and

cold stored if not frozen. And isn't it wonderful that the same has happened with all our other ingredients, too? But just as importantly, we have forums like this where we learn and share quality information on brewing.

That is a somber thought, and because of it I have worn this tie. I was the first American to be awarded this club tie from the Ealing Rugby Football Club in their over one-hundred-year history. So I wore it today as a way of saying thanks to all the wonderful guys I met at the club — David, Jack, Bob, Stuart, and all the others. Guys, thanks for the memories and for getting me into brewing. This one's for you:

"Good morning, Mr. Fisherman."
"Good morning, Sir," said he.
"Have you a lobster you can sell to me?"
Singing o-titily-o, shit or bust,
Never let your ballards dangle in the dust!

The other verses are much better. Maybe after we have a few beers at the Great American Beer Festival tonight I can be persuaded to finish that little ditty.

Now let's clean up this act. In fact, let's filter it. We might even sterile filter it. This afternoon I will be speaking mostly about the theory and practice of home beer filtration. At the end I will give you a couple methods of artificially carbonating your beer. I will also have a few comments every now and then about beer fining as it relates to making filtration an easier or more difficult process.

In some respects I feel like I am giving away some of my secrets today. I am quite convinced that a lot of my success at contests such as the one going on at this conference is because of how I treat my beers after they have been brewed and aged. As far as I can tell, filtration is one of the last challenges for the fanatic homebrewer. It is everything homebrewers don't like because it is expensive and time-consuming. But it can put your beers — especially your light ones — on a par with those of the commercial brewers. When Dave Line wrote *The Big Book of Brewing* in 1980, he said that filtration was not yet practical for homebrewers. As you will hear today, that has changed.

The Filtration Process

One of the main things filtration removes from beer is yeast. Yeast in bottled homebrew is a necessary evil. It is obviously necessary to create carbonation. But after it has done its job, things start going downhill. First, until yeast settles, it imparts that harshness and overly yeasty flavor and aroma we have all come to associate with green, newly bottled beer. Then when it finally does settle, we see an increase in yeast autolysis, or the breakdown of the yeast's cell walls. The resulting flavor impairment from yeast autolysis has been described as medicinal or as "yeast bite."

In other words, beers bottled with yeast are always going to have more of the flavors associated with yeast as part of their profiles. Again, the lighter the beer, the more one will notice this effect and regard it as a flaw or off-flavor. You just don't get those yeast flavors in commercial light lagers or light ales. Those flavors are due to our bottling with yeast. If Coors gave you a carboy of their wort pitched with their yeast to ferment and bottle prime at home, I wonder whether you would recognize the finished beer as Coors.

Filtration will allow everything the yeast produced during fermentation to come through, but it will eliminate that overt yeast character. Because of this, the first few times you filter beer, you will think you are employing some kind of instant aging process. Filtration will make your beers immediately smoother and less harsh.

But be careful. Filtration is not a substitute for aging. I remember a sterile-filtered European lager I bottled at Thanksgiving a couple years ago. I didn't think it was anything special. I put a six-pack into the root cellar and forgot about it. The following May, I cracked a bottle to taste against some beers I was thinking of entering in the AHA contest. I couldn't believe my taste buds. It was a very different beer. I entered it in the contest, and it got the highest score of any beer I have ever brewed.

You may not mind the flavor of yeast in your beer, but I will bet that none of you like oxidized beer. Filtration will not scrub oxygen from your beer. But I think it is worth adding the comment that most homebrewers' priming and bottling techniques excessively aerate their beer. Aeration isn't inherent in the process, but it is close. From the beers I have tasted lately, the number one homebrew flaw is no longer the dominating, cidery taste from the overuse of sugar in extract beers. Rather it is the tell-tale cardboardy taste associated with oxidized beer.

Because filtered beer is bottled with the proper amount of carbonation already in it, the homebrewer is able to get exceptionally low air levels in his bottled product. For example, last year at this conference I had George Fix test one of my beers with the Zahm-Nagle air

tester he demonstrated. The commercial beer he had cali-
brated the device on had 1.0 ml of air, while my beer had
0.8 ml. My point, of course, is that the bottling of carbonated beer is about as likely to exclude air as the typical
bottle priming is to include it. Bottling carbonated beer
means CO_2-filled foam bubbles completely fill the bottle's
neck, thereby purging air from the bottle's neck and giving
a defacto impact on a homebrew's taste. Note, too, that
high air levels affect shelf life as beers with high air levels
produce haze more readily.

Speaking of which, filtration also takes out chill haze,
but only if you first put it in. I want to mention that for our
ale brewers. Lager brewers form this haze as a matter of
course, unless they don't lager or age under refrigeration.
When refrigerated, polymerized polyphenols combine
with proteins — and it does take both of them, not just one
— to form what we call *chill haze*. Continued lagering will
cause these particles to aggregate and settle out.

So if you want to filter an ale at the time when you
would normally bottle, stick your beer in the refrigerator
for a day or so. You may want to do this in conjunction with
fining with gelatine or isinglass. Besides forming chill
haze, the lower temperature will also precipitate some
cold break trub. Don't feel obligated to wait for weeks until
those very small haze particles have combined and
settled. After all, that is why you have a filter. But you
can't filter out what you haven't formed. For heavens
sake, don't filter a beer cool, and don't let a beer you have
refrigerated warm up before you filter it. By doing so you
will redissolve those complexes back into the beer and the
filtration won't get rid of them.

Filtration can also be used to stabilize beer microbiologically. Large chill haze particles are only half a micron in diameter, and the tighter grades of filter pads trap them. It shouldn't be surprising that bacteria — most of which are at least twice that in diameter — can also be filtered out. Remember, too, that besides most bacteria being at least one micron in diameter, rod-shaped and spiral-shaped bacteria may be quite a bit longer than they are in diameter, so they are good targets for trapping in filter media.

I am going to add pasteurization as a final benefit of filtration. Should you want to, filtration will allow you to pasteurize your beer. Let's say you bottle a beer you really like, and you want to keep a six-pack of it for a contest a half a year down the road. Further suppose you made the beer for an occasion where it would all be consumed right away, and because of that you filtered it with a polish grade of filter pad rather than a sterile grade. The beer will appear to the naked eye to be as clear as it would be had it gone through sterile pads, but it isn't free enough of bacteria to stabilize it biologically. You wouldn't want to pasteurize a beer with yeast in it for fear of destroying the yeast cell walls. And besides, since bottle-primed beer has so much air in it, pasteurizing it will immediately ruin it by producing cooked and oxidized flavors.

Pasteurization unit (PU) tables can be found in food processing books in your library, so I won't go into how to pasteurize in a water bath. I will say, however, that studies have shown that nice, clean beers may need less than 10 PUs to achieve sterility. But most often beer is given 15 to 30 PUs. I will also add that even with the low

Advantages of CELLUPORE® FILTER PADS

■ **PREDICTABLE FLOW RATES AND PARTICLE RETENTION ... RUN AFTER RUN** A given grade of CELLUPORE® filter pad is uniform from shipment to shipment. You are assured rigid filtration quality control and economical filter cycles.

■ **COMMERCIALLY-FREE OF IMPURITIES** All Cellulo filter pads are commercially-free of leachable traces of calcium, iron and copper normally found in conventional untreated pads.

■ **WIDE SELECTION OF GRADUATED GRADES AVAILABLE** CELLUPORE® filter pads are available in a complete range of graduated grades (from No. 515 to No. 770) set to predictable standards. They give you the ability to make a pinpoint selection of the CELLUPORE® pad for optimum flow rate.

■ **PRECISELY AND CLEANLY DIE-CUT TO EXACT DIMENSIONS** Cellulo pads are die-cut to exact dimensions, with all holes and edges sharp and clean ... eliminate stray fibers and product contamination. Uniform fitting of CELLUPORE® pads assures minimum labor cost in dressing your filter.

■ **PROBLEM SOLVING** Are you experiencing a difficult filtration problem? Cellulo offers complete field service and laboratory product testing to help you solve these problems.

RELATIVE FLOW RATES THROUGH CELLUPORE® PADS
GPM/SQ. FT. @ 10 PSIGΔP — 70°F. Distilled Water

Observations:
NEXT LOWER GRADE NO. gives 50% GREATER FLOW
NEXT HIGHER GRADE NO. gives 33.3% LESS FLOW

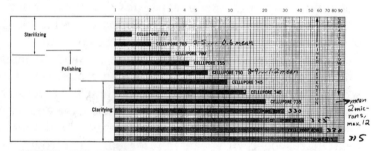

TYPICAL APPLICATIONS:

■ACIDS ■ALKALIES ■ANTIBIOTICS ■ANTISEPTICS ■APERITIFS ■BEER ■BIOTICS ■ BLOOD PLASMA ■ BRANDIES ■ CIDER ■CONDIMENTS ■COOLANTS ■CORDIALS ■COSMETICS ■ CREAMS ■DETERGENTS ■ DEXTROSE SOLUTIONS ■ DISINFECTANTS ■DRINKING WATER ■ELECTROPLATING BATHS ■ESSENTIAL OILS ■EXTRACTS ■FRUIT JUICES ■GIN ■ HAIR TONICS ■ INKS ■ INSECTICIDES ■JET FUELS ■ LOTIONS ■MOUTH WASHES ■PERFUMES ■OILS ■PHARMACEUTICALS ■PHOTOGRAPHIC SOLUTIONS ■ SALINE SOLUTIONS ■SERUMS ■SHAMPOOS ■SHELLAC ■SOAPS ■ SOFT DRINKS ■SYRUPS ■TONICS ■VACCINES ■ VINEGAR ■ VODKA ■ WHISKIES ■ WINES

COMPARE CELLUPORE® PADS WITH PADS YOU ARE NOW USING

CELLUPORE filter pads are purer and more uniform — shipment after shipment.
Request — at no charge — a sufficient quantity of CELLUPORE pads for a trial run. Send us a sample today (or give us the size, grade and accurate location of mounting holes) of the filter pad you are using now.

CELLULO COMPANY
27 North Avenue East, Cranford, N. J. 07016
(N.J.) 201-272-9400 ■ (N.Y.) 212-943-0973 ■ (Calif.) 209-485-2692
Plants: Sandusky, Ohio — Fresno, Calif. — Waupaca, Wisc.
Representatives in Principal Cities

Todd Hanson

air levels I get from bottling my beer the way I do, my pasteurization experiments have never turned out a beer as sparkling clear as those not pasteurized.

I want to mention pasteurization in association with filtration because of all the references I have been making to sterile filtration. Even though a beer may be sterile when it first comes through a pad, what about the filter housing itself, or the lines running from the filter, or the soda tank the lines empty into? Are they sterile? Then later when you bottle, are your bottles, caps, and the air floating around your kitchen sterile? So even though you wouldn't pasteurize more than a few bottles, it is not absurd to think of doing it to a beer. It is just a recognition that even though we are doing a sophisticated process, we are still doing it within the limitations of a home environment.

Homebrewers are limited to just one type of filtration — sheet filtration. We haven't the ability to first clarify beer by centrifuging it, nor do we have the kinds of prefilters that commercial brewers use before sending beer through pads like these. The big boys' last stage of filtration serves as our only stage. So let's talk about these different grades of filter pads and the physics and chemistry relative to how they accomplish their tasks.

I would like you to take a look at the Cellulo Company spec sheet shown. Take a look at the left side of the chart. There you will notice not one, but three grades of sterile filter pads. Cellulo has since added an even tighter grade, a #775. Four grades of sterile. How is that done and what does it mean for us?

For one thing, even though the name of this company is Cellulo, don't think these pads are just cellulose. These pads contain diatomaceous earth, or the silica skeletons of diatoms from Miocene-era deposits. The contribution of the cellulose to the pad's filtering ability is that it is holding the DE in place. The DE is doing most of the filtering, and there is more of it in these pads than one might think by just looking at them. For example, the #750 polishing pad on this chart contains 58 to 60 percent DE by weight, while the #765 sterile pad has another 5 percent or so DE. Then, of course, there are different grades of DE, some with smaller pore openings than others.

The interplay of DE content, DE grade, pad compression, and, in some cases, pad thickness all combine to make pads with different mean and maximum pore sizes. The #750 pad I mentioned before has an 8 to 9 micron maximum pore size and a mean pore size of 1.2, while the sterile #765 has a 3 to 5 micron maximum pore size and a mean of 0.6. In other words, the #765 pad should trap particles twice as small as the #750. I mentioned a minute ago that a large chill haze particle is only about a half micron in diameter. That should tell you what the tighter sterile grades of pads are trapping — not more yeast or bacteria, but more of those extremely small haze particles that would aggregate over extended periods of time.

This might be as good a place as any to note that when those microscopic haze particles are removed, so are some of your beer's flavor constituents. Many of you are already accustomed to this effect whether you know it or not because you are using insoluble polyvinylpolypyrrolidone, or PVPP, also referred to as Polyclar. Within two days of adding that little one-fourth-ounce packet of Polyclar to your beer, it attaches to and drops out of suspension upwards of 40 percent of the anthocyanogens in the beer. That means your beer's proteins have 40 percent fewer polyphenols to complex with and develop into haze. In addition, that Polyclar also takes out about 20 percent of your beer's isohumulones or its main bittering components. Filtration affects your beer in a similar manner. Since those microscopic protein-polyphenol compounds are responsible for some of your beer's flavor, removing a percentage of them through filtration has an impact on your beer. Most of you would be able to tell the difference between an identical ten-gallon batch, half of which was sterile filtered and half of which was polish filtered. All this means is that once you begin filtering beer, you will find yourself modifying any long-held recipes to counteract filtration flavor losses.

Pads trap material in two ways, the first being on the basis of the tortuous path the particles take as they are pushed through the pads. One can imagine a yeast cell squeezing down a pore, flowing along a cellulose channel, changing directions, and then suddenly being forced up against and caught by a particle of DE. There it stays, perhaps itself serving to trap other particles behind it. Eventually the yeast, bacteria, and chill haze of a given diameter are caught. Eventually, too, the channels through the pads become plugged. In a moment I will discuss how much beer one can expect to get through these various grades of pads before they become plugged.

But first, another way these pads filter is through adsorbtion. That is with a "d," not a "b." The pads have a slight positive electo-static charge, and yeast, bacteria, and protein have a negative charge. So in some instances, particles that are small enough to get through a pad cling, or adsorb, to it anyway.

One will offset this adsorbtive effect by running a beer through the pads with too great a pressure differential between beer in and beer out. I personally don't ferment my beers under pressure. Since I don't have to worry about back-pressure to keep CO_2 in my beer as it goes through the filter, my pressure differential is always identical to the pressure I apply to the beer going into the filter. This differential is best kept to 10 psi or less, though I have to admit I have cranked up the pressure in my filter to 15 psi rather than not getting the last gallon of a beer through the pads. Unless you are sterile filtering, I wouldn't worry too much about exceeding that 10 psi differential by a few more pounds. But if your beer is flowing nicely at 5 psi through the pads, don't crank it up to 12 to get the job done more quickly. Keep good notes on pressure and filtration times so you can start making assessments about how such factors as aging time, yeast type, and the finings used affect the length of your filter runs.

Home Filtering Beer

That is what filtration does for your beer's flavor and stability and how it works. Now let's talk about the actual filters and their operation.

Whereas a commercial plate-and-frame filter would use any number of pairs of filter pads of much larger size, the most common filters we have available to us use only two pads. This is the seventy-five-dollar Vinamat wine filter from Denmark that I am currently using. The beer enters the filter between the two pads through a hole in the center plate, pushes outward, and is collected and channeled out via the grooves on the two halves of the frame. The filter comes with a six-liter plastic reservoir with a hand pump built into its cap to generate pressure for the filter, but for filtering beer, you might as well forget using that plastic reservoir. It would need to be filled three times for one five-gallon batch, which is bad for oxygen pick-up, sanitary reasons, and your sanity. Rather push the beer from a stainless steel soda tank under CO_2 pressure to another such tank.

The pads themselves should first be flushed with water before you start running beer. They should also be sterilized. I accomplish these both at once by running five gallons of boiling water through the filter, an operation which takes about ten minutes. This boiling water doesn't hurt the pads, but it is rough on the filter. These stainless steel tubes are replacements for the original plastic ones that behaved like spaghetti during the hot water flush. I am also very close to having ruined this housing. After the hot water softened the housing, the pressure distorted the frame's original flat surface between the reinforcing ribs into one resembling that of a tilt-a-wheel carnival ride. There is no help for this one, but if I bought this filter new, I would pour an epoxy or plastic resin into the spaces between the frame's exterior support ribs so the entire surface is supported better and less likely to flex out of shape. Then again, maybe this bowing won't hurt a thing since there is a reinforcing plastic ring on the housing where it counts — around the outside edge where the plate and frame seal against the pads.

Maybe the best solution is to buy a better filter if you

can afford it. The Michael Joseph Company in Buffalo, New York, makes a top-notch filter with almost the same number of square inches of filter area as the Vinamat, but constructed of a plastic resin designed to be steam or hot water sterilized. It is a sturdy unit with a more commercial, square design that lets one add plates without making the simplest version of the filter obsolete. Their "Duo" model is the equivalent of the Vinamat and sells for about $120. They are currently supplying Cellulo pads at the same price as the round pads the Vinamat uses — about $1.20 apiece. I will soon be retiring my Vinamat to my father's wine cellar, where the rigors of boiling water flushes aren't necessary, and buying a Michael Joseph filter.

You will notice that after that water flushing, the first couple quarts of beer run through the filter must be discarded. For one thing, there is a slight but noticeable flavor from the DE in the pads, which is released when the pads are hot. Plus, the first runnings are especially subject to that adsorbtive effect of the pads, so they have far less flavor than the later runnings.

But these two concerns can be remedied. I am proud of devising the following step, so listen carefully. To avoid wasting a couple quarts of my beer, I waste a couple quarts of someone else's! Go to the liquor store and buy a case of ye olde $3.99 special. Cool down eight of them — three quarts of beer — and use them for filter fodder. You will love it. It is fun to open eight beers rapid fire, but if it still breaks your heart to throw away those eight beers, here is what you do. Take a sip of the last one going in and think of how much better yours is. That will make you feel better!

But the important thing is that you run some beer through the filter at about 5 psi to cool and acclimate the pads. A commercial variation of this procedure would be to run some cold, sterile water through the pads after the hot water and before the beer flush. That may save you a few bottles of beer flush, but it will cost you some time in the kitchen the day before. When finished flushing with beer, continue pushing just CO_2 for a minute to get most of that beer out of the pads and to purge the system of oxygen. By preflushing the pads in this manner, you may only throw away a pint or so of the filter's first runnings of your beer rather than upwards of two quarts. But use your old taster to guide you as to when you want to begin directing your filtered beer into your soda tank.

Whether or not you are sterile filtering, you will want to be careful about the sanitation of the tank you will be filtering into. I have had good luck sanitizing well with a strong chlorine solution, rinsing twice with hot tap water including, of course, the draw tube. After running the second rinse out the tank's syrup line under pressure, I don't open the tank anymore. When I am ready to run the beer into it, I do so via a fitting attached to the tank's quick-disconnect syrup line. I loosen the gas line fitting to provide for release of CO_2 in the tank as it fills with beer. This is a cleaner method than just opening the tank's lid and dropping the filter's out line to the bottom.

If you brew five-gallon batches, both the Vinamat and Duo filters are entirely adequate. The pads they use aren't so large that you would be wasting a lot of their filtering capacity by running only five gallons through them. In fact, these filters are even fine for someone like me who brews in fifteen-gallon batches, but only because I am an experimenter and will split that fifteen gallons into two or three different experiments that I will filter separately. At most I have wanted to run ten gallons through one set of pads. Good thing, because these pads couldn't handle a fifteen-gallon polish filtration.

What can filters handle? Here are some observations. If you want to get to a beer very quickly — and when you get a filter you will do that, you can push five gallons of twelve-day-old lager through #750 polish filter pads. To do that particular trick, you cannot secondary ferment. Rather you must do what the big brewers do — primary ferment on the high end of the lager temperature range until fermentation is complete, wait a couple days after fermentation is done for the yeast to reabsorb diacetyl, then rack and refrigerate the beer for two days with your finings to chillproof it and drop just enough yeast out of suspension to let you get it through the pads.

I don't recommend you do a lot of that kind of brewing, but I thought I would mention it because you lager brewers know how turbid a twelve-day-old beer is and can use that as a gauge to how much muscle this size filter has. On the other hand, if you give your lagers a more traditional six weeks or more in the secondary and fine them well, you should be able to run ten gallons through a pair of polish filter pads.

Sterile pads are another matter. Remembering that the #765 sterile pads have pore sizes half that of the polish filter pads, you have to have a pretty clear product going in if you expect to filter even five gallons. That is just for the 765s I personally use. I couldn't tell you what to expect if you went to a finer grade of sterile, but I would be hesitant about using too tight a grade. Given all the extra

Todd Hanson

work and expense of filtering beer, I can't say I would be too thrilled about polish filtering a beer first so I could then run it through really tight sterile pads. Nor would I be too happy about running two-and-a-half gallons through tight sterile pads only to have the pads get plugged, forcing me to either bottle the rest immediately or repack and reflush the filter to do the other couple gallons.

Ways to Home Carbonate

Let's move on now to carbonation. There are so many ways to carbonate beer that it would take an entire speech to discuss all of the variations brewers use. Instead of doing that, I thought I would just mention some principles of gas laws and give you a carbonation formula I have recently worked up with the help of a physics teacher colleague of mine. This formula will give you brewers who have messed around with artificial carbonation a new degree of consistency. For those of you who have never carbonated beer with CO_2 pressure, this method is ideal because all it will cost you is a couple beers for one of your friends in the restaurant or bar business. All the necessary equipment — including the CO_2 — can be borrowed. You don't even need a CO_2 cylinder to bottle the beer once it is carbonated.

The carbonation method I want to suggest to you is what one might call the "big-bottle-of-beer" method because we are going to carbonate the beer in our soda tank as if it were one big bottle of beer.

I have here an unopened, properly chilled bottle of commercial light lager. This brewer has put what he feels is the correct amount of CO_2 in this beer. When I shake this bottle of beer, does it still have its correct amount of CO_2? That is a little bit of a trick question. I used to be a high school teacher, so my lifetime contract says I am entitled to ask one of those every now and then. The beer in the bottle does not now have its correct amount of carbonation because I have shaken a lot of it out of solution. Yet in another sense, it does, because the bottle has its correct amount of carbonation. The cap is still on. Even though I have caused some of the beer's carbonation to be released into the bottle's headspace, if I put this bottle back in the refrigerator for a couple days, the CO_2 will again reabsorb to a level no more nor no less than before I shook it.

Conceivably I might have been able to shake every bit of carbonation out of the beer in this bottle. If I did that, I should be able to find some device to measure the pressure in the bottle's headspace. Knowing that, if I had another bottle with exactly as much dead beer in it as this one contains, I could theoretically carbonate it to an identical CO_2 volume level by capping it with an identical head pressure of CO_2 because that high head pressure would absorb into the beer.

I don't know of any way you can do that with a glass bottle, but you can do it with a stainless steel vessel able to withstand almost nine atmospheres of pressure. That is what I have worked out in the computer spreadsheet I worked up. You don't need a computer to do these computations, but if you transfer the formulas to a spreadsheet, it will allow you to change variables and get new results right away. That is important because these tanks have a maximum working pressure of 120 pounds per square inch, and if you have too much beer in the tank, you won't be able to carbonate to the higher CO_2 levels. This is done at Standard Temperature and Pressure. I filter at 32 degress F or sometimes at 31 degrees F, but I will get into that later.

One-Shot Beer Carbonation
CO_2 Injection Computation

Variables
A Headspace in tank (ml): 3150
B Equilibrium CO_2 (psi): 11.0
C Beer to carbonate (ml): 15624
D CO_2 volume level desired: 2.80
   Ales, keg: 0.8 - 1.3
   Ales, bottled: 1.5 - 2.2
   Prem. lagers: 2.3 - 2.5
   U.S. lagers: 2.5 - 2.8
   Wheat beers: 3.8 - 4.9
(Note: assume .25 vols CO_2 will be lost during bottling process.)

Computations
E Total ml Headspace: 6453
F Grams CO_2 required: 85.00
G Ml CO_2 at STP required: 43270.5
H Atmospheres required: 6.7
I PSI to apply: 109.6

Converting Liquid Level to ML
J Inches of beer: 16.875
   (from tank's bottom to nearest 1/8")
Equivalent ML:

K   22" alloy: 16014.5
L   23" alloy: 16014.5
M   23" alloy: 15624.2

Spreadsheet Formulas

A - Headspace in excess of 5.0 gal. (use chart)
B - Tank equilibrium pressure after maximum CO_2 absorbtion (use chart)
C - Beer to carbonate (use inches-to-ml conversion chart)
D - Level of CO_2 desired
E - 18,927 - C plus A
F - {(C x D) / 5.147} / 100
G - {(22.4 x F) / 44} x 1,000
H - G / E
I - (H x 14.7) plus B
J - Length of tank's "sweat line" from base (to nearest 1/8")
K - 3785.334 + (J - 5.125) x 1211.307
L - 3785.334 + (J - 5.125) x 1211.307
M - 3785.334 + (J - 5.5) x 1211.307

Figures Used

18.927 Ml in 5.0 gal
5.147 Conversion factor for changing CO_2 volumes to CO_2 weight
22.4 Liters in 1 gram molecule
44 Molecular weight of CO_2 molecule
14.7 Psi in 1 atmos.
5.125 Inches from base of tank required to reach 1-gal. level
5.5 Same as above but with tank of different manufacture
3785 Ml in 1 gal.
1211.307 ML in every 1 " of tank height given a standard

Todd Hanson

cylinder
inside circ. of 28 1/4

Headspace in Various Tanks in Excess of 5.0 Gallons
22" alloy: 2000 ml
23" alloy: 3150 ml
23" Firestone: 3150 ml

CO_2 Equilibrium for Desired Volume Level

Volume:

1.75	1
1.85	2
1.95	3
2.05	4
2.16	5
2.27	6
2.38	7
2.48	8
2.59	9
2.70	10
2.80	11
2.90	12
3.01	13

Basically, the computations in this formula combine various known values — such as the volume of headspace in a soda tank, the volume of beer we have to carbonate, the weight of a mole of CO_2 gas, and the pounds per square inch pressure of one atmosphere — to let us calculate the head pressure needed for our giant bottle of properly carbonated beer.

This is a perfect system except for one thing. CO_2 goes into ice cold beer quite rapidly at high pressures, so I can't tell you how much CO_2 is absorbed between the time you start pressurizing the vessel and the time you unsnap the quick-disconnect fitting. That may result in a higher volume level than the formula says, but then again you will lose around 0.25 volumes of CO_2 during the filling operation. To minimize this effect, turn your regulator up to the pressure you will be inserting into the soda tank and do the CO_2 injection on the quick side. As soon as the flow of CO_2 starts slowing down, unsnap the gas. If you leave the gas line attached to the tank, the regulator will keep on hissing quietly, signifying that the beer is absorbing CO_2

Once you have injected CO_2, shake the daylights out of that tank for a half a minute or so. Rather than shaking CO_2 out of solution at this stage in the process, you will instead be shaking it in by exposing the gas to a greater liquid surface area.

Precautions for Carbonating

There are a few precautions for using this procedure. First, be sure not to exceed the maximum working pressure of the soda tank you are using.

Also be sure to purge the headspace in your soda tank of any air before pressurizing it. If you don't, you will void your beer of the benefits of air exclusion this method gives you. Turn the pressure in your regulator up to, say, 15 psi — about one atmosphere — and fill the headspace. Then release all the pressure. According to Boyle's Law, doing that once will dilute the air in the headspace by 50 percent.

Doing it twice will dilute it down to 25 percent, and so on. The greater the headspace in the tank, the more important this CO_2 purging is. Go ahead and waste the CO_2 at this point. It is cheap after all you have been through with your beer.

Remember that this method must be done over at least two days' time. CO_2 dissolves more slowly the closer it gets to its equilibrium pressure, so unless you have a pressure tester to use in conjunction with a CO_2 equilibrium chart (such as the one in last year's *Beer and Brewing Vol. 6*) to monitor the tank's pressure drop, wait at least two days before you bottle beer carbonated in this manner.

Finally, when bottling carbonated beer, do not draw it through the quick-disconnect fittings that come on these tanks. They will do to your carbonation level what shaking the bottle of beer did before. Rather, remove the quick-disconnect springs and washers and pins from both the tank's syrup line fitting and any fittings that attach to it. This is something to also keep in mind if you use these tanks as draft units. Removing the quick-disconnect mechanisms will not break your pressure seal; the o-ring seals the two fittings, not the quick-disconnect mechanisms. Removing those innards gives your beer a straight shot from the draw tube through the fittings to your tapper without any unnecessary turbulence and carbonation loss.

A beer picnic tapper replacement hose clamped to a quick-disconnect fitting is the way to go if you want to bottle carbonated beer on a regular basis. One costs about fifteen dollars from a beer distributor and lets you control beer flow very well. Plus you can use it in a draft set-up.

I promised this would be a cheap method of bottling, so don't be afraid to use a length of siphon tubing pushed onto a male barbed soda fitting to get your carbonated beer from the soda tank to your bottles. The draw tube in the soda tank is not used in this method. Carbonate your beer without it, or remove it just prior to filling. Simply attach your tapper hose or tubing with barbed fitting to the tank, remove the tank's other fitting, and position your tank horizontally a couple feet above your work area. Gravity flow will get the carbonated beer into your bottles. This gravity flow method actually fills bottles better than if one used a pound or two of CO_2 pressure to push the beer up the draw tube from the floor to your work area.

Don't worry if after running the beer down the tilted sides of your bottles you can't fill them all in one shot. Either set them aside and top them up a couple minutes later when the foam has subsided, or force fill the bottles to the desired level. Even high-volume beers should not cause you to backlog more than five to ten bottles in your filling line. Of course, always bottle your beer at the coldest temperature possible to minimize off-gassing.

Speaking of temperature, note that this carbonation formula is designed to work at Standard Temperature and Pressure (STP). STP is 0 degrees C and one atmosphere pressure, so if after filtering your beer it has warmed up a bit, go through your CO_2 purging routine and put it back in the fridge for a few hours to get it back near 32 degrees F. Then shoot it with the correct amount of CO_2 pressure.

There is another method of carbonating beer I would like to share with you briefly today. It is an elegant little system for carbonating and bottling beer at the same time devised by Mike Caldwell (for more information see chapter on Trends and Innovations in Brewing Equipment). Ads for Mike's system have appeared in *zymurgy* under the name of the Carbocap Carbonator.

Basically Mike's system collects CO_2 either from primary fermentation or from a sugar water and yeast generator and stores it in a mylar balloon for later injection. A special screw-on cap with a one-way gas nipple has been designed to work in conjunction with the disposable plastic bottles the soda industry uses. A hand pump draws CO_2 from the balloon and injects it into the cold beer, while the cap keeps it from escaping. After every few pump strokes you shake the beer and you can actually feel the pressure in the bottle lessen as the CO_2 dissolves into solution. One can vary the CO_2 volume level by varying the number of pump strokes. When you've shot the beer with CO_2 disconnect the pump and the beer is carbonated for immediate consumption or storage like a regular bottle.

It is a simple, straightforward method that accomplishes the same major benefit the method I use does — a significant reduction in air levels for a much more stable product.

Todd Hanson has been an avid homebrewer for thirteen years. He was formerly a journalism and broadcasting instructor in Sheboygan, and is now pursuing his interests in the homebrewing and microbrewing industry.

Julius Hummer is happy brew-master of award-winning Kessler Bock.

9.
Brewing to Scale
How Batch Size Affects the Finished Product

Finn Knudsen,
Adolph Coors Company, Golden, Colo.

Today, I will discuss the topic "Brewing to Scale." The presentation consists of a number of slides that will give you an idea of various-sized installations and the problems involved in producing identical products in small-, medium-, and large-size breweries. During the presentation, I will be referring to the brewing, fermentation, aging and finishing processes.

The food and beverage industry has always had problems in trying to scale processes up or down for products with complex flavor profiles. Many professional people believe, or have believed, that it is easy and possible to produce the same product in large-scale or small-scale breweries alike, utilizing the same process parameters. However, homebrewers, microbrewers, pilot brewers and commercial brewers have all found this not to be the case. Similarly, the multi-plant or international brewers also experience problems when trying to match products from different brewery installations, especially during start-up conditions. But they overcome these by relying on experienced technical staff and sophisticated laboratories to

Finn Knudsen

meet all in-house specifications and consumer evaluations.

Even when plants are built exactly the same, some differences may still occur. Some of the differences are because of the design of, and materials used in, pipelines; the way the mixing takes place in the kettles; the yeast and wort handling; the operations of the fermenters; the relationship of exposed materials to the beer in transport between vessels; and so on.

Here I will attempt to cover some information on typical sizes and their related problems.

What Is the Definition of Scale?

In general, the brewing industry has reported the

following definitions:
* microbrewery - up to five liters,
* minibrewery - up to twenty-five liters,
* pilot brewery - over twenty-five liters, with the majority around a hundred liters,
* commercial brewery - larger than a pilot brewery, such as 400 hectoliters, for example.

At Coors we have available a three-liter microbrewery, and we also have a pilot brewery that is one-sixteenth the size of our commercial brewlines, or thirty-plus barrels.

What Is the Purpose of the Pilot Brewery?

The main purpose is trying to duplicate the function of the commercial-scale units and trying to produce enough beer for analyses and flavor evaluations. In most cases, this objective has been modified to being able to produce a product again and again; in other words, the reproducibility became its purpose rather than trying to duplicate the existing commercial facility. Then, when that was achieved, the focus again was turned to making beers that taste the same as the production beers. In doing this, all brewers have found out that the process parameters have to be changed. For example, people brewing in 100-liter brewhouses often get diacetyl off-flavors in the beer during the fermentation process, even though they did not have that problem in the larger commercial scale. The only way they could get rid of the off-flavor was to change the fermentation-maturation temperatures.

Well, you might ask, if a brewer cannot copy a product in a pilot brewery, then what can he find out about the beer? Remember, the point is to be able to reproduce a brewing process over and over again. The pilot brewery brews the identical beer time and time again. At that point, the pilot brewery really becomes a research facility. Because then the brewer can vary his brewing, fermentation and aging parameters. He can then try different types of raw materials, different new products, and so forth. With this information he can start correlating his processes to those in the large brewery, and trying it on the large scale to see if he gets the same results.

What Is Impacting Brewing to Scale?

Raw Materials

Water, as you all know, is very critical to the brewing processes, and varies from location to location. If you as a homebrewer move from one area to another and try to brew the same beer, you will find that it has changed character because the water composition in your new home is different from that of where you lived before.

Another example is barley malt. Bill Coors has a nice saying about this: "Barley malt is really the single most important ingredient in beer. What grapes are for wine, barley is for beer." In your case, if you use malt extracts or syrups, you will find differences in them from time to time and batch to batch, even though you are always buying from the same supplier. You think the malt and syrups you buy always are the same, but they aren't.

Hops are another example, both raw hops and pellets. Hops deteriorate with time. If you want the same hop character from your hops over a period of time, hop extract probably is one of the better ways to go.

Finn Knudsen

Brewhouse

The pilot brewhouse at Coors has the same type of vessels as those used on large scale, and the same type of mash filters. As I mentioned, everything has been designed at one-sixteenth scale, so we can actually try out different brewing processes and monitor them. Brewing at the size of thirty to forty barrels, a brewer can copy to a great extent what is happening in the commercial-size brewhouse. But still the brewer must consider that the grind being used is different, and the stirrer and vessel are smaller so the exposure to the metal in the container is much different. Also, the way the mash is mixed in the kettle is different from the way the malt particles are being handled in the commercial kettles. The only way we can hope to steer these processes is by having good process control of the pilot brewery. In that way we can continually repeat the processes — even down to our mistakes. For this reason our pilot brewery has very fine controllers, as has our microbrewery.

One brewer in Switzerland with a 20,000-barrel brewhouse makes two brews a day, five days a week, fully controlled by a computer. The process is very precise, and even the hops are added automatically from a carousel containing measured amounts of hops, which automatically dumps them into the kettle at the right time.

Another example is the Swiss Brewing Research Station in Zurich, which has a one-hectoliter pilot brewery. It is used to simulate different kinds of brews for the breweries in Switzerland. None of the breweries there have any research facilities, so they have all invested some money into this one common facility at the research station where investigations can be conducted.

After the brew has been made, it has to be cooled, and this is where most homebrewers — as well as many large brewers — make their major, first mistake. It is during the cooling process, when the wort is exposed to air or unprotected, that there are a lot of possibilities for microbial contamination. This contamination is very easy to detect because it can be tasted before the beer is finished. Unfortunately, at that point, it is too late to rectify the mistake. When you taste or smell strong off-flavors in your beer, it is better to dump it and make a better brew.

Another place where strict control must be exercised is in the aeration of the wort. The 20,000-barrel brewery in Switzerland mentioned earlier has a whirlpool, wort chiller, and aeration system — all completely closed. At the pilot brewery at Coors, we also have a whirlpool tank, a plate heat exchanger, and an air tank for aeration — also a completely closed system, which is the best controllable system you can work with.

Fermentation

In the fermentation process, the brewers in the good old days kept different yeast strains in different wooden vessels. From there the wort went into open fermenters, exposed and very likely to pick up wild yeast and bacterial infections during the fermentation. Yet, these open fermentation systems are still in use in many small European breweries today.

In our pilot brewery, we have four fermenters that are ten-barrel. They are part of a closed system, and here again, we copy as much as possible the liquid depth, etc. that we have in our regular fermenters. We want to simulate the processes we use in production.

At Carlsberg's one-hectoliter pilot brewery, the beer is put into four small fermenters of twenty-five liters each, and cooled in a waterbath. The brewers control the fermentation temperature to plus or minus one-tenth of one degree Celsius. During their start-up of the pilot brewery, they had a lot of problems with formation of diacetyl flavors when using the same time-temperature process in the pilot fermenters as was used in the production vessels.

In order to control the temperature of a homebrew batch, one homebrewer wraps his old shirts or coats around his five-gallon container to maintain a good, solid temperature during fermentation since he has no other means available. At the Coors microbrewery, we use glass flasks for fermentation, and we can accurately control their temperature with a waterbath.

Aging and Finishing

In the past, cold cellars were used to age or finish the beer. Some small 150-hectoliter cellars are still in use in many places in Europe, and they still produce good, decent beer.

At the Coors pilot brewery, we have ten-barrel aging tanks. We can experiment with counterpressures and liquid levels to get more or less the same environment as is in our regular aging tanks. We recently insulated our tanks for better temperature control and also have experimented with low temperatures during aging.

At the Swiss Brewing Research Station, the fermenters and aging tanks are the same size as the brews. Counterpressure on these tanks simulates the hydrostatic pressure normally found in regular-size aging tanks. At Carlsberg, there are twenty-five-liter aging tanks, maintained to within one-tenth of a degree temperature control during aging. These also have counterpressure possibilities.

In doing a mini-brew, one homebrewer uses a five-gallon keg. When the beer is ready for aging and finishing, he siphons it out into a keg. Then he puts the beer into a home-modified refrigerator. The beer cools and clarifies for a week or so and then can be dispensed from a tap mounted on the front of the refrigerator. This brewer has arranged his brewing schedule so he always has fresh beer available from the tap.

In the pilot brewery we use an Enzinger Mass filter. We don't pasteurize our beers, but filter our beer to sterility. Of course, if you don't keep the beer clean up to this point in the process, and you have had microbiological infections, you cannot filter out the off-taste that has been caused by the microbes. You may be able to filter out the organisms, but you cannot remedy flavor problems that occurred during fermentation and aging by filtering the beer.

There are other filters such as sheet filters, available for small breweries. Using these, the brewer can simply put counterpressure on a keg with beer in it, and then push the beer through the filter into another keg. Of course, this is after the brewer has cleaned and sterilized the equipment by soaking everything in Rapidyne, for example.

Let me remind you that it is very important that you keep all your equipment very clean. Most, if not all, problems that homebrewers face have been caused by microbiological contamination. If you keep your equipment clean and sterile, you can avoid this. Other off-flavors can be caused by the hoses and plastic containers you use. In very heavy, high-gravity beers, you may not taste them as much as in the lighter products, where off-flavors come through very strongly.

You may think that you will not have problems with plastic, food-grade hoses and pails, but try soaking the hoses or pails in beer, and then tasting if the beer has off-flavors. I strongly recommend that you only use glass-ware, and that if you do use plastic material, you do the flavor evaluation mentioned above.

Serving the Beer

How you serve or pour your beer depends on how you like it. Personally, I like the method an old brewmaster taught me twenty-five years ago. He demonstrated pouring the beer down in the center of the glass so that a nice head developed. Thereby, a lot of the coarse bitterness is removed. Then, drink the beer from under the foam, and when all the beer has been consumed, there should still be some foam left. When the foam has settled, try tasting it, and you will know what he meant: the beer becomes smoother when the coarse bitterness is removed in the foam.

Different styles and types of glasses are available as per your preference: tall and thin, or mugs. Some mugs have covers, and one may wonder why. It is recorded that the old Babylonians used mugs with a cap or cover so that when they walked to the brewery and filled their mugs, the cover would keep dust and other particles out of the beer while they walked home.

In closing, please try to think about the processes and the equipment you are using for production, and be aware that you never really can copy a commercial beer as homebrew, if you wish to do so — even when you have the recipe. Only when you change the process parameters will you be able to come close. Keep the equipment sterile and clean, and try to avoid plastic off-flavors by selecting inert equipment.

Bibliography

1) Ahrenst-Larsen, B. (1967), "Nyt Forsogsbryggeri paa Tubory," Brygmesteren.

2) Hahn, Charles W. and Coors, Jeffrey H., (1975), "Design, Construction and Start-up of Pilot Malting, Brewing and Storage Facilities," Vol. 12, No. 4, MBAA Technical Quarterly.

3) Hug, H. and Pfenninger, (1977),"Uberprufung der Reproduzierbarkeit von halbtechnischen Brauversuchen und der angewandten Analytik," Schweiz. Brauerei Rundschau, Jg. 88, No. 6.

4) Hurlimann, Martin, (1984), "Das Buch Vom Bier," , Switzerland.

5) Marchbanks, Chris, (1897), "Avoiding the Pitfalls when Brewing on a Small Scale," Brewing and Distilling Inter-

national.
6) Pfenninger, H.; E. Schlienger, F. Ullman and R. Schur, (1970), "Die neue halbtechnische Brauerei der Verschsstation Schweiz. Brauereien." Schweizer Brauerei-Rundschau, April.
7) Thomas, D. A., (1986),"The Magic of Malt," Beer and Brewing Vol. 6.
8) Verlagshaus, Rosenheimer, (1980), "Bierkrug-Deckel", Alfred Forg Gmbh & Co., Rosenhein, Germany.

Finn Knudsen earned his M.Sc. in Chemical Engineering from the Royal Danish Technical University in Copenhagen. As Director of Research and Development at the Adolph Coors Company in Golden, Colorado, he has overseen such special projects as the development of the highly successful Winterfest Beer.

Andy Thomas shares his award-winning Thomas Kemper Helles.

10.
From Concept to Concrete
Confessions of a Homebrewer-Turned-Microbrewer

Jon Bove
Maine Coast Brewing Company, Portland, Maine

Did any of you see an issue of the *Wine Advocate* last fall? In it was a guide to the world's 300 greatest beers, and the author said that until he had tasted some of those, he had never considered beer more than Sunday afternoon swill. He said, "I realize, after 300 beers, that I have to consider my beer palate a lot like my wine palate. There's as much complexity in good beers, as in good wines."

Best of all, he was nice enough to include Portland Lager in his list of the world's great beers. I would like to read you the review: "Portland traditional lager, Portland, Maine. Medium-amber with a creamy head; fruity malt aroma; good intensity; crisp entry; medium bodied; smoothly textured; very rich, flavorful palate; nicely balanced; and good length." Those are all adjectives I would like to claim for myself, with the exception of the fruity aroma.

It is true that our beer has quite a bit of flavor. We use Hallertauer and Tettnanger hops and a blend of four malts made up for us by Briess Malting Company. We have been contract brewing for a little over a year. Basically, we have a very small company; there are four partners and one employee. We have been low-key, but have done very well, and our beer is distributed around New England and a little bit beyond — to Colorado, for example.

Jon Bove

I guess I began in this business seventeen years ago when I flunked second-semester Russian because someone had given me a copy of the *Mother Earth News* a magazine that said you, too, could brew beer for only pennies per gallon. Between the time my roommate and I read that article and the time we skipped out on our final exams, we were averaging about twenty gallons per week output from our dorm room. I remember that it was somewhat humorous to watch those of us who were just back from Southeast Asia twitch and look nervous whenever the bottles blew up under the beds. Those were happy times, we think, although truthfully, few of us remember them.

Before then, my only previous experience with fermentation was when I was a merchant sailor. Then, there was a ship's baker from Jacksonville, Florida, who concocted something for us when we were crossing the Pacific called "five-day wonder," the less said about which, the better. He could certainly have been found guilty of fruit abuse for what he brewed, and certainly of crew abuse.

The other day I ran into my old college roommate, and

he remarked that it was nice to see me doing something productive for a change. Beyond that, he reminded me that we used to slouch in our chairs and say, "Gee, wouldn't it be nice someday to have a little brewery?" I finally ended up with a degree in Japanese, with commercial brewing the furthest thing from my mind, although I was still homebrewing. Through the 1970s and early '80s, I pursued various careers in radio advertising, sales and restaurant management. Ironically, I think that all of those things provided me with skills that have helped me with the brewery. In 1982, I found myself running a gorgeous, little federalist-mansion-turned-banquet-hall, and doing very well. But I was still an employee — and a lousy one. It was a little like chapter four of *Passages,* where the author describes how a young guy hits his early thirties, and feels he has to make his mark.

Because I was married to a woman from the San Francisco Bay area, I was traveling there quite a bit, and seeing the new breweries pop up. Anchor Steam beer was everywhere, and I had a six-pack of New Albion. I caught wind of Dr. Michael Lewis' seminars on microbrewing in the spring of 1983, and decided to go ask questions and see if I might want to get involved in making good beer and selling it to the public. That year, the Sierra Nevada people spoke at the seminar, along with Jim Schlueter, who owned the now defunct River City Brewery; reps of Robert Morton Ltd. from Burton-on-Trent, England; and some marketing people.

They thoroughly presented the problems: financing, used vs. new equipment, quality control, price competition, distributor relationships, recipes, etc. But they did make having a brewery sound feasible. They made it sound as though the little breweries that had had trouble were too small, too underfunded, or both. They made it sound as though if you ran your brewery as a real, professional business, it was something that you could do. They gave the impression that there is a future in the industry for the craft brewer.

Of course, I thought I was smarter than anyone else, and began putting together a business plan and raising money. I thought that I knew all the power people in Portland, Maine, and that I could throw together a quick plan, take it to the guys, and have all the money I would need to get the brewery going by fall of 1983. I borrowed a computer from a friend and started doing cashflow planning. My wife and I went to England and toured small breweries and visited Robert Morton to look at equipment. We also visited with Tim O'Rourke, who was born in a brewery and had a degree in brewing sciences.

We decided that we wanted to develop a New England regional brewery. By that, I mean a fifty-barrel brewhouse, with maximum capacity of about one million cases a year, in a 20,000-square- foot building. We wanted to brew a lager because we felt there was room for one. The craft brewers then were not producing lagers, and we felt that there was a reason why the whole world, with the exception of the United Kingdom, switched to lagers in the mid-1800s. We felt lager offered a rounder, smoother taste, with complexity yet balance. We decided to produce a very high-quality lager, which we would call Portland Lager, and also reserve the option of putting out specialty beers like ales or stouts.

The size of our projected brewery was partly dependent on the fact that it is difficult, when you're much smaller than fifty-barrels, to get bottles. At that time, glass suppliers didn't want to talk to you unless you were buying 100,000 bottles. We also felt it was as easy to make fifty barrels as it was to make twenty barrels. We wanted to avoid seasonality in our beer market. Maine is a very seasonal state; people flood it during the summer, but it is absolutely dead in the winter. I wanted to try to have urban sales in Boston and Hartford to carry us through the winter. Maine is like the Oregon of the east in some ways; it has a reputation for clean air, clean water, lots of space and independent people. For this reason, we felt that the image of a Maine beer would probably do well throughout the rest of New England. These were all good reasons for building a regional brewery.

It looked like we would need about $1,250,000 to pull it off. We settled on Robert Morton equipment, and Tim O'Rourke signed on with us as a consultant to help with beer recipes.

By then, my business plan was over a hundred pages. I started meeting with bankers, the Small Business Administration and accountants with allegedly good contacts. The financial people told me I would need an independent market study before I would be able to raise the money. So I hired a market consultant and had a survey done that cost $6,500 and told me that yes, Mainers would be interested in trying a new, local, high-quality, regional beer. Surprise! I thought it was naive, but it impressed the financial people.

We got into high gear and hired new lawyers who specialized in dealing with the SBA and lawyers who specialized in dealing with investors. We were trying to get a bank to finance the maximum amount that the SBA and state would guarantee — about $800,000. That would leave us about $500,000 to raise through equity investors, and we felt that we had a substantial supply of investors just waiting in the wings for us.

We found a bank that accepted our proposal. Its voting board approved our loan, and I immediately went to the lawyer and committed $15,000 in nonrecoverable legal fees to make an offering to the investors. Then we went happily went to California for Christmas vacation.

We returned to Maine buoyant and confident, and found that the bank had merged with another bank, and the new board had reneged on our deal. At that point, I was penniless — we had put all of our money into the brewery, including money we had borrowed — and felt that our plans were done for. I couldn't find another bank that would lend to us. I knocked on venture capitalists' doors, but they were still into losing money on high-tech.

Then, someone wrote a newspaper article about me in the Portland paper, and prospective investors began calling, one of whom was Hugh Nazor, who is currently my partner. He was in his late forties at that time, had an MBA, had made his money in the electronics field, and was semi-retired. Also, he had been a homebrewer for twenty years and had entertained thoughts of opening a local brewery, but didn't want to expend the energy to do it by himself. The reason he got involved was that he was sailing down the Maine coast and ran into some people who told him about a fellow in North Carolina who had fixed their boat for free and said, "When you come back from Maine, bring me some of the local beer." They had to bring him Moosehead.

He became an active partner and put his considerable

financial skills and some money into the business. We started a fresh effort in 1985. We applied for an industrial revenue bond to the city of Portland, which would grant us tax-free status. We shopped that around to the banks, and everyone thought we were nuts. One of the standard ways of raising money in an equipment-intensive business like brewing is to ask equipment manufacturers for a guarantee that they'll buy your equipment back at 75 percent of its new value, if necessary. But in this new, emerging industry, we couldn't find an equipment company with enough financial strength to give that kind of guarantee.

We were thorough and aggressive in presenting ourselves (our business plan was up to 300 pages), but ultimately we simply were not able to convince people in Maine to back us. Finally the idea for doing a contract brew revived.

We always had wanted a brewery in Maine. I think that if we originally had wanted to do a contract brew, we could have had it on the market by 1984. But, we had come up against an immovable brick wall. We decided we could prove ourselves more thoroughly to the investment community by getting a beer on the market, and having it brewed in another state was better than nothing.

We began renewing contacts with regional breweries and settled on the Hibernia Brewery in Eau Claire, Wisconsin, as our contract brewer for various reasons. It was a small brewery, extremely willing to work with us, with good people, who had won awards at the Great American Beer Festival with their all-malt beers. We wanted a brewery with real experience in making the all-malt-type beers because these beers are so vastly different from the pale, American, adjunct beers. We wanted a fairly well-balanced product with a lot of hoppiness and a lot of malt body to carry it through.

The mad dash began at the end of October 1985. In 120 days, we contracted with Hibernia, perfected our recipe (a compilation of input from Tim O'Rourke, Hugh, myself, our other partners, and Hibernia), and got our label, artwork and packaging together. My wife and Hugh's wife then began taking active roles in the brewery. We had computer-generated critical path charts to tell us what we must do in order to accomplish what we wished. We decided against hiring an ad agency because of the cost, and because we felt that the attention we'd give it was worth several ad agencies. I spoke with over a hundred distributors in New England, and whittled the choices down to seventeen.

We spent about $200,000 in four months doing all this. In our first month of sales, we sold just about that much. It was a thrill! Maine being the world's largest neighborhood, I was the media darling. I was on every television station, in every newspaper, the topic of press conferences.

Then reality struck in April. It was mud season, and we realized that New Englanders don't drink beer during mud season. All the Bud drinkers who switched to Portland Lager went back to Bud. We were the eighth largest shipper of beer in Maine in March 1986. In April, sales plummeted. Fortunately, summer came, and sales went back up. From this we learned many things:

• that we had to market our beer;

• that the taste of our beer was going to be its prime selling point, but the word had to spread to a larger group of people;

• that distributors had more on their minds than our little company;

• that we needed a stronger presence with retailers.

We didn't want to be trendy. We didn't want to climb up to the top of the pyramid and then get knocked off by the next trendy beer. We wanted to build our drinkers one at a time. So we hired a young woman to represent our beer in Boston first, and then throughout New England. Portland Lager began getting some very good critical reviews. When we came to the Great American Beer Festival in 1986, we were the naive sheep without give-aways and professional models to represent us. But even without all the electioneering gimmicks, Portland Lager still placed fifth. We believe this was directly attributable to its taste.

We have also learned some hard lessons, one of which is that table tents do not stay on restaurant tables and bars, and therefore your beer is at the end of a list of twenty beers that may or may not be mentioned by the waitress. In summer of 1987, we will come out with a draft beer.

We are now going through a massive shift: we are moving our contract from Hibernia to F.X. Matt in Utica, New York. We have had no real problem with Hibernia, but it costs us $1,000 less to ship from Utica to New England, and we need to save our pennies. Matt also gives us the capability of draft beer. We want to be part of the spiel when the waitress says, "On draft, we have...."

Also, we have come out with our first big, point-of-sale piece — a five-case bin for the package stores in Maine.

The investors and bankers are much more positive

about us. They see our beer in the package stores and that impresses them. I don't think we will have to beg for money in the future. We are now negotiating for an absolutely gorgeous old mill on the National Historic Trust, about forty-five minutes north of Portland. It is in a small, economically-depressed town where there's a chance of state help for start-up. The mill is on a river with waterfalls, and part of the brewery will be on an island with a walkway over the river. We just got the Maine law changed regarding a brewery serving beer. Before now, the brewer could not legally have given a sample of his beer, nor have even tasted it himself. Nor could we have had a pub. But now, we can give samples of our beer, as well as have a pub. We would like to have nice, little textile mill museum, and offer a tour of the brewery. We are about fifteen minutes from L.L. Bean, so we will be able to blanket the area with signs saying "Free Brewery Tour." Our pub will be inexpensive, and we want to feature all Maine products: cheeses, wines, smoked meat, etc. There is also space in the mill for shops and a hotel.

What is the ultimate moral of this story? It has been five years of my life now, and I still don't have a brewery. It is stunning! I have spent five years just to come to the point where I can brew beer. If any of you are thinking about building a brewery, think about that.

If I were to do it over again, I don't know how I would do it differently. The awareness of the craft beer industry is much larger, now. Things have changed. For example, whiskey is going down the tubes in sales now, and a major "brown goods" house approached us with an offer to buy the business. They told us that they see craft beers as the only area of real, major industry growth potential. In retrospect, I think I would have started the contract beer right off and quit screwing around with financial people.

Also, I would have been more cohesive in my promotion with the distributors. The distributors practice double-speak: they tell you they will promote your beer aggressively, when in fact, they go back to selling Bud in a few days.

I would have gone out and gotten $100,000 in seed capital from the start. I bankrupted myself, which was nuts.

Ultimately, making beer is a fun business, which provides some returns.

Q: Have prices changed much since when you first started?

JB: The figures I had for building then are almost meaningless now, things have changed so much. At that time, a Robert Morton turnkey brewery with a fifty-barrel, three-vessel brewhouse was about $800,000, including bottling, installation, shipping, etc. With currency changes and inflation, that cost probably has doubled now. I couldn't go to Robert Morton now. We have someone piecing equipment together for us from various sources. I believe we will be able to put the equipment for a fifty-barrel brewhouse together for approximately $800,000, although I can't be too specific.

Q: Could you talk about the cost dynamics of contract brewing? For instance, do you buy the ingredients?

JB: It varies from place to place. It behooves you to shop around because the various breweries quote a price based on what they will provide and what you will provide, such as packaging materials. We are switching over to used, brown, twelve-ounce, Miller bottles. We will get them from our distributors for fifty-five cents a case, and use them once. They will have to be washed, of course. The brewery handles the acquisition of malt.

Q: How can you control quality when you are a long way from the contract brewer?

JB: It is a problem, but it is possible. You can have your beer analyzed by a lab on a regular basis. Or you can spend quite a bit of time at the contract brewery, like our partner Hugh did. You can have samples of your beer shipped to you before the load is trucked. But overall, we had a good relationship with our contract brewery, and it lived up to what we were looking for.

Q: How did you decide on a recipe for your beer?

JB: We did test brews at Briess Malting Company, and also in England with American ingredients. We had a good idea of what we were looking for, and then we ran test brews at Hibernia until we got the beer we wanted.

Q: This is a suggestion. Wherever you go in the country, ask to see the beer list. If everyone does this, we will educate people to serving different kinds of good beers.

JB: You are absolutely right. Every month in New England, there are a hundred new beer lists. In some cases, we are paying for the printing of beer menus, and I know that some other companies also are doing so.

Q: How did you develop the motif for your packaging?

JB: The lighthouse (shown on the label) is the single most evocative symbol of Portland, Maine. As far as the label, we felt that every label in the beer coolers is designed to shout at you. We wanted to go the opposite, and to provide a place where your eyes can rest. Basically, the four partners just hammered it out.

Q: What is your shelf price in Maine?

JB: Around $5.25 for a six-pack. We sell about 5,000 cases a month in New England, and Maine is about a quarter of our sales.

Q: How did you sell the distributors on your beer?

JB: With a great deal of enthusiasm, although I believe they liked the flavor and packaging. Also, we tried to listen to what they said they needed. If they speak double, as I mentioned, that means you have to listen with both ears.

Editor's note: The historic mill that Maine Coast Brewing was about to move into burned to the ground on 23 July 1987.

Jon Bove received a B.A. in Japanese in the University of Massachusetts and is co-onwer of Maine Coast Brewing Company, producer of the successful Portland Lager.

11.
Making Homebrewers
Creating Interest in Homebrewed Beer

Daniel Bradford,
Association of Brewers, Boulder, Colorado

How many people here are commercial brewers? How many are potential commercial brewers? It looks like about one-third commercial brewers and one-third amateur brewers. I'd like to address my comments to both groups.

What I mean by "making homebrewers" has to do with sharing your passion for beer. When I first started working with the Association of Brewers, I probably had logged a total of two-and- a-half cases of beer in my life. But since then, I have become a beer junkie. I am definitely addicted; beer has definitely become a vice. The prevailing argument I get at home is, "When are you going to clear out all of these beers?"

We have three refrigerators now, all filled with beer. I also have a closet where one would normally stash garden tools, that is filled with beer. As a matter of fact, my idea of a good time is shutting off the computer at eleven o'clock each night, turning on the television to any movie, getting as supine as I possibly can, and pouring myself a nice, thick stout, strong ale, porter, or barley wine. So what I would like to talk about is how I have changed from being someone who considered beer undrinkable to being a beer junkie. I bet that at least 95 percent of the people in this room share that passion. The other 5 percent are probably accompanying, if not supporting, an addict.

I believe that the love of beer unites us. As near as I can tell, there are three things that create this love

Daniel Bradford

— one of which is the inherent beauty of beer. With each year, I get a little more interested in wine and single-malt whiskey, but only because I understand them better through beer. The beauty of beer is undescribable, and drinking a beautiful beer is beyond compare.

The second thing that creates this love is the simple pleasure of drinking a beer. One of the finer moments in my odyssey towards addiction came after I produced my first imported beer festival, which makes the Great American Beer Festival seem like a tame event. It was an international beer tasting with no budget, and more than 170 beers. Around midnight after the event, after cleaning up and moving out all the product, I went to the stash, grabbed a bottle at random, sat down under a pine tree under a full moon, and rediscovered British ale. Just the sheer pleasure of that moment further pushed me into my vice.

The third thing we all share is the camaraderie of beer. When wine people get together, they have what my father referred to as a "pissing match" of knowledge. Scotch and whiskey people don't get together. Your average typical gin drinkers wouldn't know that they were together. But beer drinkers, on the other hand, like to drink beer together. There is nothing that compares with getting a group of friends together and passing around some beers. Camaraderie is drinking and talking beer.

In making homebrewers we must remember that beer has talkability. You don't often discuss the history, advertising strategy, fermentation times, and recipe changes of any other beverage but beer. Of all the beverages, except for that brief flurry about classic versus new Coke, beer is the only one that inspires passion in knowing the drink's history.

Then there is the culture of beer. I associate beer with parties, while some people might associate it with baseball. There is a whole culture that goes along with beer. Unlike soft drinks, wines, or single-malt whiskeys, beer does not stand alone; it has a cultural heritage.

Then there are the aesthetics of beer, which we love to talk about. The aesthetics of beer are just amazing.

But in making homebrewers, what is the mission of beer? In my involvement with several nonprofit organizations, I am very sensitive about creating mission statements. I conclude that the mission of beer — not brewers — is passion, affection, love and talkability. So that is our task. As lovers of beer, our task is to fulfill the mission of beer: to communicate our affection for beer and its talkability.

One tactic for doing this is to promote beer history and

breweriana. Tactic number two, which unites all of us here, it to make beer, whether we are commercial brewers or amateur brewers. In producing the Great American Beer Festival, I have the honor of working with virtually every commercial brewer in the country, several of which serve as my mentors and influence my passion for beer. The inspiration that Fritz Maytag, Bert Grant and Jim Koch provide us with is simply incredible. Passionate commercial brewers go out and talk beer to the public. They talk about their motivations in making beer, about beer ingredients, about their methods of brewing, and most importantly, they talk about their pride in making beer. This is how commercial brewers fulfill the mission of beer.

At the Great American Beer Festival, we have 180 volunteer servers who are charged with one, primary responsibility: to ask people to think about beer. When we ask people to begin thinking about beer, we are on our way to making converts and to fulfilling the mission of beer.

For homebrewers, performing this task is more difficult than it is for commercial brewers. Ninety-nine out of 100 media believe that homebrew is green, believe that homebrew explodes, believe that homebrew breaks up marriages, believe that homebrew was responsible for the premature death of their grandparents, believe that homebrew is one of nastiest things you can do and you do it in your basement and don't tell anyone. There was recently a very nice article about Catamount Brewing Company in *Time Magazine*. The reporter readily understood microbrewing, but then wrote two throw-away lines about homebrewing that took us right back to the 1920s and '30s. So in order to fulfill the mission of beer as homebrewers, we have a difficult time.

There are ways we can fulfill our mission, however. We can show people that homebrewing produces quality beer. I spent a weekend with Byron Burch of the Sonoma Beerocrats, and over the two days we were together, we sampled thirty different homebrews that could easily have been sent to the European Brewing Conference to compete on an international level on quality. I am so audacious as to say that I believe homebrewers are making the best beer in the world at this time.

Beyond quality is the variety of homebrewed beers. At the 1987 Great American Beer Festival, a professional panel comprised of seven members of the brewing community judged the Festival's 120 beers. This was a singularly awesome event because it was the first time in the country that it has been attempted. Still, we had only twelve commercial styles. Yet at this year's National Homebrew Competition, which is the largest in the world, there were over seven hundred entries representing twenty-six beer styles. The American Homebrewers Association officially lists thirty-five different styles. We need to tell people that not only do we make great beer, but that the variety is incomprehensible.

We also need to tell people that homebrewing is simple. My favorite opening remark to reporters is, "Let me tell you about my five-minute beer." A former homebrewer of the year and I are going to work up an article called "High-Speed Brewing," describing how fast, we can make how much beer, that is how good. I used the cold-water method for making a Mountmellick stout, following the directions; it was made in five minutes and was very good beer. I just emptied the can in, poured the water in, put the yeast in, and put the top on. At the other extreme, Byron Burch can work a day-and-a-half to produce one batch. Statistically, about 60 percent of the beers that members of the AHA make are made in forty-five minutes. That is: extract, with some grains added for body or color. We need to let people know about the simplicity of making beer.

The fourth factor, which is not as significant in the United States as in Canada, is the economy of brewing your own beer. We can make some of the world's best beers at some of the world's cheapest prices. You can't match the price of a homebrew, and the gratification, which we all know to be very real, is a freebie. We need to let people know that we can make beer for about thirty-five cents a bottle, once we have our start-up.

Finally, we need to let people know about the pleasure of homebrewed beer. Each year, I gather together about six people to help me produce the Great American Beer Festival, and I bring them over to my house for a beer tasting. While we are tasting beer, we make a batch, and they are just astounded how we casually make five-gallons of beer. We need to communicate the quality, variety, simplicity, economy, and pleasure of beer.

So how do we make homebrewers? First, we have to bring beermaking out of the dark ages. A person should never have any sense of reluctance about homebrewing. There should never be any linkage to bathtub gin or granddaddy's days. We should never talk to the press about "the good old days." That produces the downside.

Second, we need to give our craft some class: we do, in

Daniel Bradford

fact, make the finest beers in the world. We can position ourselves as such. We need to redefine homebrewing as something that gives exquisite pleasure. It is enjoyable; it isn't just a bunch of good-old boys sitting around, whipping up some brew. We need to adopt a pursuit-of-excellence approach; that is, brewing for excellence. For example, the Sonoma Beerocrats are the most award-winning group in the country. Byron Burch says that it is the "top-gun" approach that does it. He inspires a spirit of amiable competition among his brewers to see who can win at competitions, or who can make the best beer.

Where shall we make homebrewers? Through the media. We have a story that the press still doesn't believe, and we have a golden vehicle to make them believe it: a beer. You can get many reporters excited about what you are doing by giving them a beer. If all of you were to go back to your hometowns, write up a detailed description of how to drink homebrew, and waltz into every television station and newspaper in your area with it, I bet that at least one-third of you would come up with a television or news story about beer.

Or we can approach organizations. The Rotary, Kiwanas, Elks, Optimists and Chambers of Commerce have potential homebrewers in them. When you get home, volunteer to give a brewing demonstration at club meetings. If you mention that you want to talk about tasting beer, not drinking beer, you will certainly have a forum.

Another opportunity for spreading the word is at liquor stores. How many of you work closely with a prominent liquor store to promote beer awareness? These guys are looking for ways to sell beer, and we are looking for ways to get people excited about appreciating beer.

Retailing a beer and homebrewing a beer go hand-in-hand. Just invite the liquor store manager to your home to make beer, or offer to educate his staff about beer appreciation. This can work with restaurants, beer distributors and breweries.

We are, in fact, a community of brewers; from August Busch to Charlie Papazian, we all share the same goal. If we all work together on that goal, we can start turning the public on to our passion. And if we succeed in fulfilling our mission of beer, beer might do us the favor of not giving us any more hangovers.

Daniel Bradford is the marketing director for the Association of Brewers, and the brains behind the promotions, public relations and membership drives for the various departments of the Association. He is also director of the Great American Beer Festival, and an inveterate lover of good Bock.

12.
Yeast
How Different Types Affect Beer Flavor

George Fix, Ph. D.
Arlington, Texas

In putting together the material for this talk, it became apparent that there are three general points I want to make. I will make these points at the beginning, and then the remainder of my presentation will be a series of examples that are designed to illustrate and clarify the points.

The first point, and perhaps the most transparent, is that yeast is the most delicate, and therefore, the most critical ingredient in beer. As I go through the examples, I will not bother to keep making this point because it is so obvious.

The second point deals with the way we categorize yeast. There is the historical tradition where yeast strains have evolved from what we now called "baker's yeast." There also are the geographical differences in the evolution of yeast. And of course, the biologists have gotten into the fray with various ways of classifying yeast. All this is extremely important and interesting, but its relevance to brewing is marginal. The central point is that each particular brewing strain that is available to us has its own unique personality. Each of these personalities differ dramatically — as dramatically as the personalities of the people in this room, which is no small statement at an American Homebrewers Association Conference. If you leave this presentation with any one thought, I hope it is a sense for the enormous diversity in yeast strains. The diversity is sufficiently dramatic that classification schemes, while of interest, are not what we should focus on. It is the individual personality of these strains that is most crucial.

Dr. George Fix

The final point is that healthy, viable yeast are, in fact, the brewer's best friend. In this point I am referring to more than their ability to ferment our worts, without leaving behind a lot of nasties in the process. They protect our beers in really important ways. The moral of this is: yeast are certainly worth whatever time and attention we give to them.

These are the three main ideas I hope emerge from my examples. Now I will turn to making these points in terms of specific yeast strains. The only significance of the yeast strains discussed is that I have good data on them from both commercial and amateur brews. Also, I have included enough strains to give you a sense of the diversity.

Whitbread

The yeast from Whitbread is a mixed culture. It has a big, generous personality. From an article I read, I believe that mixed cultures such as this are losing favor. This is a shame for the unique flavor profiles produced by mixed cultures cannot be matched by single-strain cultures.

Sierra Nevada

This strain was cultured by Phil Dillon from a Sierra Nevada Pale Ale bottle, and it is Sierra Nevada Brewing's production yeast. It is neutral in terms of personality, which means it brews clean beers where the malt and hops do all the talking. It is highly recommended. Thanks to people like Phil, Y-East Lab in Oregon, and others, getting access to yeast like Sierra Nevada is now a viable option for homebrewers.

Anheuser-Busch

I included this strain to make the point that just because a yeast does very well in large-scale commercial brewing, it does not mean that it will necessarily work on a smaller scale in either homebrewing or microbrewing. This is Anheuser-Busch's production yeast, and has a lot of interesting characteristics. As a whole, however, its performance in small-scale brewing has been disappointing.

Sierra

The fourth strain makes the reverse point: just because a yeast is successful in large-scale brewing doesn't mean it can't be successful in small-scale brewing. This is the yeast that is used to ferment Samuel Adams, and is Pittsburgh Brewing's production yeast. This yeast also has been highly successful in small brewing.

HW

Since most homebrewers don't have access to Sierra, I am including this example as a yeast that is "user-friendly" to small-scale brewers. This one also was cultured by Phil Dillon, one of North America's great yeast enthusiasts. It came from Spaten's bottle-conditioned wheat beer. Spaten's primary fermentation is done with a top yeast — one well-known for producing phenols and a clovelike flavor, which is not the one you want (except for wheat beers!). As customary now with most of the German wheat beers, the secondary bottle fermentation is done with a "lager yeast," which is this one. Its performance has been highly satisfactory in small-scale brewing.

Weihenstephan 308

This is another German yeast, and it is a typical problem yeast. It is a yeast with an enormous personality, and it is very "user-unfriendly." It is one of the most frustrating yeast strains I have ever encountered. In fact, the people who have to work with it on a daily basis have renamed it "Wisenheimer 308." Sierra Nevada and HW try their best to adjust themselves to your brewing environment, provided you take care of them, keep them well-fed, and keep them away from infection; "Wisenheimer," on the other hand, does nothing to accommodate your conditions and demands that you adjust to it.

Yet, in three competitions, four homebrewers took five first-places, two second-places, and three best-of-shows with seven beers brewed with Wisenheimer. I don't pretend to understand this, but it does raise questions about the difference between good competition beers and good drinking beers.

Now I would like to discuss the personalities or profiles of these yeast strains and illustrate their differences. First, I will quickly discuss in general terms how a yeast strain ferments. I will touch on attenuation, flocculation, the preferred fermentation conditions, and most important, stability with respect to mutation.

Whitbread

Culture — Whitbread is a mixed culture consisting of three strains. Two are fermenters, one a flocculating strain at the end of fermentation and one with no sedimentary properties. The third strain, very common to traditional English brewing practice, is a "chaining yeast," as it is called in the British literature. A chaining yeast does nothing during fermentation, but its genetic structure is such that it strongly flocculates at the end of the fermentation. These three strains work together to produce a mildly flocculant yeast.

Stability — Mixed yeast cultures are highly praised in English brewing in comparison to the continental single-culture strains because they are very stable with respect to mutation. This is certainly the case with Whitbread. I had a culture going for eight years until I lost it when I moved from Pennsylvania to Texas. It is a very stable yeast that will not mutate under normal conditions.

Temperature — The preferred temperature is 60 to 65 degrees F (16 to 19 C). Whitbread is sensitive to temperature, and if it gets colder than that, it starts to shiver and becomes inactive.

Attenuation — Whitbread, like many top yeast, does not ferment as completely as lager yeast. In particular, it does not ferment minor wort sugars such as melibiose. In practice, it will incompletely ferment trisaccharides like maltotriose. Thus if you were to take a generic all-malt wort at 12 degrees Balling and 1.048 specific gravity, it would generally take it down to 3.5 or 1.014. In comparison, a lager yeast would go down further.

Sierra Nevada (SN)

Culture — The Sierra Nevada yeast is a single strain.

Stability — Its stability is excellent.

Temperature — Part of Sierra Nevada's "user-friendly" attribute is that it is very insensitve to temperature. SN ferments commercially at between 60 to 65 degrees F (16 to 19 C), but I have seen it ferment at 50 degrees F (10 C). In fact, it can be used as a lager yeast in the traditional process where the partially fermented wort is racked over and undergoes a secondary fermentation at 35.6 degrees F (2 C).

Attenuation — SN ferments completely. A biologist would say that an ale yeast cannot ferment these minor sugars, but Sierra Nevada completely ferments melibiose and maltrotriose and other trisaccharides, very much like a lager yeast strain.

Anheuser-Busch (AB)

Attenuation — AB is a flocculant yeast.

Stability — This yeast has very nice properties all around, except for one main problem: it has a very strong propensity for instability. Anheuser-Busch grows all its yeast in St. Louis and ships it to its regional breweries. Then after the yeast is used four times, it is disposed of and new yeast is brought in. AB needs to do that to maintain product quality. This is the problem in using this particular yeast in small-scale brewing: it mutates. Usually two to three times is all you can expect.

Temperature — The desired temperature is 54 degrees F (12 C).

Sierra

Sierra has a far different type structure.

Attenuation — Sierra is a mildly flocculant yeast with a slight powdery character.

Temperature — A lot has been made of fermentation temperatures. New Amsterdam Amber, for example, made with this yeast, is fermented at 65 degrees F (18 C). Samual Adams, on the other hand, is fermented at Pittsburgh Brewing at 62 degrees F (17 C). As a third example, some homebrews ferment at 50 degrees F (10 C) with this strain. The differences between these three fermentation temperatures in terms of the production of esters and other important qualities are minimal compared to other yeast strains. Sierra can withstand different fermentation temperatures and keep its personality intact.

Stability — Sierra could be used for three or four hundred fermentations without mutation. It is very stable, but once mutants become present, they cannot be washed out.

HW

HW, the yeast from Spaten, is excellent, just like Sierra Nevada.

Attenuation — HW is a good fermenter with good sedimentation properties.

Temperature — It is primarily used in the cold range for fermentations from 48 to 50 degrees F (8 to 10 C).

Stability — It is very stable with respect to mutation.

Wisenheimer 308

You can ferment this strain at the usual 50 degrees F (10 C), but you will wish you hadn't. The only way we have ever been able to partially harness Wisenheimer 308 is with a Narzsis-type fermentation. This is a new scheme developed in Germany. You start cold, say at 48 degrees F (8 C), until approximately 67 percent attenuation has been achieved. At that point, you turn off the cooling and let the wort warm up over a twenty-four-hour period to 65 degrees F (19 C). You hold it at that higher temperature until the fermentation is complete. Then the temperature is dropped to 37.4 degrees F (3 C) for a twenty-four-hour cooling period before racking.

Wisenheimer also absorbs large amounts of sediment — wort trub, excess hops, etc. This can impart a bitter flavor that can be filtered out to some extent. It also can be reduced by washing yeast in a tartaric acid-sterile water solution at a pH of 3.0 every three brews.

Washing does damage to the yeast cells, so the first fermentation may be disappointing. The second fermentation, on the other hand, is usually sensational. Then on the third, you start picking up the trub again. So Wisenheimer produces one good beer out of three. It is indeed a frustrating yeast!

Now I want to continue with the second part of my presentation, discussing these yeasts in relation to:
• Fusel alcohol, Fatty acids and Esters;
• Diacetyl; and
• Sulfur compounds.

Fusel Alcohols

These are the alcohols in beer other than ethanol. They are produced in a very different way: ethanol is a result of a metabolism of wort sugars, while fusel alcohols come from the metabolism of amino acids. The details aren't important; what is important is that each individual yeast strain has some options in how it ferments. In particular, each of the yeast strains discussed have their own propensity for creating fusel alcohols. High fermentation temperatures and high wort gravity add to the effect, but the yeast strain is dominant.

Fusel alcohols have strong flavors. Whereas ethanol has a flavor threshold of 15,000 parts per million, fusel alcohols are generally detectable at 100 parts per million.

They also are more intoxicating and toxic then ethanol. In addition, fusel alcohols play a negative role in beer staling in that they can be oxidized to unpleasant aldehydes.

Fatty Acids

Here we are talking about the caprylic-type acids that yeast purposefully and deliberately produce during fermentation. If the production of fusel alcohols is one aspect of a personality of a yeast, then the production of fatty acids is the second. Fatty acids produced via yeast metabolism have unmistakable soapy/fatty/goaty-flavored constituents.

These are not the only fatty acids in beer; for example, wort trub contains complicated, unsaturated fatty acids. They also play a role in beer staling, along with the fusel alcohols, but they are not related to yeast metabolism. Another type of fatty acid that has nothing to do with yeast is responsible for the cheesy flavors that result from oxidized hops.

Esters

Esters are what tie all this together. I have data on many beers, and I haven't seen one where esters haven't been an important component of the beer. If they were removed, the beer would change. In fact, on a priority basis, the major contributors to beer flavor are ethanol, hop bitters, and then esters.

An ester is a combination of an alcohol and an acid, and it is a characteristic of the yeast strain that stimulates the production of esters from these components. Of course, brewing conditions also play a major part. For example, in high-gravity brewing, ester levels increase as the wort's starting gravity is increased. In fact, once you achieve a certain level — around 12 degrees Balling — the rate of ester production also increases.

There are ninety different esters that can occur in beer, but let's look at just a couple that are most important. Amyl acetate is called the banana ester because of its flavoring. It is strong, with a threshold of 1.3 parts per million. It is a combination of amyl alcohols and acetic acid.

Ethyl acetate is a combination of ethanol and acetic acid, and has a threshold of 35 parts per million. It gives a fruity tone that sometimes can take on a solventlike character.

Let's now see how the different yeast strains behave with respect to the production of selected fusel alcohols, fatty acids and esters. In discussing these matters, it is important to keep in mind that the key parameter is not the level of the constituents, but the ratio of it to its threshold. This is generally called the Meilgaard Flavor Unit.

Whitbread

The Whitbread strain produces a tremendous amount of esters. For example in the Whitbread Extra Pale Ale, the banana esters are over three times their threshold (see the chart below). The International Bittering Unit (IBU) of this ale is about 30 ppm. Since threshold of the hop bitter (the alpha acid) is around 10 ppm, it, too, is around three times its threshold. This results in an aroma that is an unmistakable blend of malts, hops and bananas. As can be noted from the chart below, ethyl acetate is present at its threshold and comes up in the background as a fruity backup to the banana aroma. Ester data from selected small-scale brews tend to be close to those of the commercial ale.

In the commercial product, the fatty acid level is 8 ppm, which is near the threshold of 10 ppm. The two fuel alcohols listed in the chart (i.e., the amyl and phenol alcohols) have similar flavor units. The fact that they are not major constituents (i.e., having flavor units of two or higher) is a reflection of the Whitbread strain's propensity to convert them into esters.

Sierra Nevada and Anheuser-Busch

The SN and AB strains are similar in the sense that the fatty acids and fusel alcohol levels are low, while the esters are at or slightly below their thresholds. This is typical of neutral yeast, and they tend to produce beers where the malt and hop character dominates over any fermentation characteristics. The data shown in the chart are for Budweiser in the case of the AB strain, and selected test brews in the case of SN.

Sierra

Sierra is a yeast that produces esters regardless of fermentation temperature. We measured the ethyl acetate level at 38 ppm in New Amsterdam (denoted NW in the chart). In the Samuel Adams (denoted SA), it is slightly less at 35 ppm. Test brews fermented at 50

George Fix

degrees F (10 C) averaged around 34 ppm. The net result is a gentle fruity flavor tone.

HW

The HW strain has characteristics very similar to Sierra. It is a fruity yeast and gives a nice, gentle note to the beer.

Wisenheimer

Wisenheimer 308 is remarkably neutral in this area.

Table 1

| | Fusel Alcohol | | Fatty Acids | Esters | |
	Amyl	Phenol	Capric	Ethyl Ace.	Amyl Ace.
Thres.	(110)	(100)	(10)	(35)	(1.8)
Whitbread	138	60	8	36	8
SN	70	30	<5	26	1.8
AB	59	32	<5	16	1.4
Sierra	62	25	<5	38 NA	2.0
				35 SA	
				34 CF	
HW	65	40	<5	30	2.1
W 308	55	15	<5	25	1.8

Note: all figures refer to ppm.

Diacetyl

I do not believe that diacetyl production is part of a strain's personality. As a normal part of fermentation, yeast produce a-acetolactic acids. Some of these interact with amino acids inside the yeast cell, and others just leak out into the fermenting wort. If air is present, they will oxidize to diacetyl. This process is enhanced as the fermentation temperature is increased. Bacterial activity, high air levels, and poor wort composition are also factors.

Where the biggest difference in yeast strains occurs is in their ability to reduce diacetyl. Normal yeast contain specialized enzymes that reduce diacetyl to harmless diols. The strength of these enzyme systems varies with different strains.

Diacetyl Levels
Table 2

WB	0.09
SN	0.05 - 0.08
AB	0.06 (but is 0.2 - 0.3 with mutation)
S	same
HW	0.05
W308	0.25 - 0.3 at normal fermentation
	0.10 - 0.15 at Narzsis fermentation

Whitbread, Sierra Nevada and HW

These strains are excellent diacetyl reducers, and the commercial products brewed with these yeast typically have low diacetyl levels. The same was experienced with small-scale test brews, the only exception being cases when technical errors occurred (most notably high air levels), which is not the fault of the yeast.

George Fix

AB and Sierra

Both of these strains are good diacetyl reducers until mutations occurs, when the opposite is the case.

Wisenheimer

Wisenheimer presents a major problem. If you were to ferment Wisenheimer in the normal way, you would get diacetyl levels around 0.25, which you could taste. The point of the warm period at the end of the fermentation in the Narzsis procedure is to assist in diacetyl reduction. Just as diacetyl production is increased with increasing temperature so is diacetyl reduction. Most strains do not require the warm period, but Wisenheimer certainly does (or equivalent procedures).

Sulfur Compounds

You will hear many different opinions on this topic because the data are very inaccurate. I will confine my attention to Dimethyl Sulfide (DMS) because it is relatively well understood and important.

Sulfur components in beer typically have low thresholds, and in the case of DMS, it is 50 parts per billion. The precursors of DMS are found entirely in malt. They are S-methylmethinine (SMM), and Dimethylsulfoxide (DMSO), the oxidized form of DMS.

There are various mechanisms that bring about DMS. Under heat, SMM can be converted to DMS in the kettle boil, most of this being washed out with evaporation. This conversion also takes place during wort cooling, and some literature suggests that this is where the major DMS level occurs since there is no generally evaporation. Long wort cooling times, therefore tend to produce high DMS in wort.

DMS is reduced in fermentation, as it is mechanically scrubbed out with CO_2 evolution. I believe there is evidence to show that yeast cannot product DMS. I once thought that DMSO was reduced to DMS in the fermentation, but it has now been conclusively shown that that cannot happen in beer wort. Yet yeast do apparently differ in their ability to reduce DMS, a process that is not very well understood

Bacteria can produce DMS. They also produce hydrogen sulfide and the net effect is rotten-vegetable flavor tones.

There is very little DMS in English ales. The reason is that English malt is kilned at a very high temperature, which in effect removes the DMS precursors. Most English ales have DMS levels around 15 parts per billion, which is well below the threshold. Where the controvery comes is in lager. The DMS levels in many European lagers can run as high as 75 to 100 parts per billion, where the net effect is a malty, slightly sulfury tone. In fact, DMS levels are often used as a flavor discriminator between ales and lagers.

National beers in the U.S. rarely have high DMS levels. In fact, a recent report from Anheuser-Busch declares that DMS levels above 50 parts per billion are, by definition, a technical flaw. Some regional beers in the Midwest run DMS levels in the range of 50 to 75 parts per billion because of high SMM levels in midwestern malt.

DMS Levels
Table 3

WB	<50 ppb with English malt
SN	<50 ppb with most malts
AB, HW, S	<50 ppb with U.S. two-row malt
W 308	100 - 125 ppb with most malts, especially U.S. six-row

Whitbread and Sierra Nevada

The ale yeast, at higher temperatures, scrub DMS right out of the wort. Both the Whitbread yeast and SN yeast, according to my data, have no sulfury characteristics.

AB, Sierra and HW

These are relatively weak reducers of DMS. If midwestern malt is used, a slight sulfury tone may be detcct able.

Wisenheimer

Wisenheimer is a highly sulfury yeast. Coming out of fermentation, you get virtually the same amount of DMS as when you started. This produces an extremely intense malt character.

Summary

In conclusion, I feel that beer clubs are going to play a very creative role in maintaining yeast. I suggest that you try getting a very stable yeast like Sierra Nevada or HW and keeping it on cold wort between fermentations, instead of beer. The amount of wort is not so important, but you must make certain that the yeast is constantly fed so that it doesn't deplete the fermentable sugars and the amino acids. If you constantly feed the yeast, you can go weeks, maybe even months, between brews. Sierra Nevada has been kept intact for years under the process. Obviously, keeping clean and sterile conditions is critical.

As another point, I have seen how dry yeast are produced. My other talks have been very negative about dry yeast, and now that I thoroughly understand the process, I am absolutely negative. The technology of drying yeast in an oven is primitive, to say the least. I asked why these producers don't use liquid nitrogen to freeze the yeast dry, and they told me that then they couldn't sell it at fifty cents per packet, but would have to charge more. I believe it is our fault that we give such a low priority to our most critical ingredient, while we spend many dollars on malt.

George Fix Ph.D. is a professor of chemistry in Arlington, Texas. A homebrewer and member of the Master Brewers Association of the Americas, he has written numerous brewing articles and is regarded as an expert of brewing topics. His valuable research has benefited brewers nationwide.

13.
Folklore of Beer in America
A Look at Beer Breweriana

Will Anderson,
Portland, Maine

How is everybody doing this morning? At a beer convention you never know! I suspect that we all had a brewski or twoski last night!

I am going to be talking about beer and America. When I was asked to speak about beer and America, I thought back to last December when I still lived in Brooklyn. The section of Brooklyn in which I lived was called Park Slope — because it sloped from the park — and the local newspaper was called The *Park Slope Paper*. They sent a reporter over to interview me about my book, *Beer USA.* It made the front page with a headline "Slope Man Says Beer Is What Made This Country Great" and pictured me with a bottle of Yuengling's celebrated Pottsville Porter in one hand and a hot-off-the-press copy of *Beer USA* in the other.

Frankly, I didn't say that beer was what had made America great. What I did say was that beer-drinking people tend to be temperate people — as opposed to wine-drinking people, vodka-drinking people, or rum-drinking people (which is what we were until the British cut off our

rum supplies from the West
Indies during the Revolu-
tionary War). And temper-
ate people tend to be indus-
trious and prone to making
pretty sane and sensible
decisions.

The article, however,
made me think about the influence beer has had on
America, and how it has influenced our culture and way
of life in some specific ways.
It made me wonder what if
beer hadn't arrived on the

Will Anderson

scene. How would our lives be different? Today I want to
talk about three or four examples of this influence, which
I call, "What if?"

What If? Number One

For my first "what if?" I will go back 120 years to the
year 1867.

That was the year Colonel Jacob Ruppert was born.
He was not born a colonel, of course, but he was born into
affluence, and a family that encouraged him to pursue his
many and varied interests. During the course of his
lifetime, the Colonel was into collecting jade, porcelain,
bronzes, fine art, rare books, yachts, race horses, Indian
artifacts, and just to add spice to his life, monkeys. He also
bred prize St. Bernards, was a member of many, many
social and business clubs and associations in and around

New York, and, of course, very successfully ran the family brewery, Jacob Ruppert, Inc. The Colonel's greatest love, however, was baseball. He was an avid fan almost from the time he was old enough to be able to tell a ball from a bat. He spent many an afternoon at the polo grounds watching his beloved New York Giants play (back in the years when the Giants were where they belong in New York, instead of in San Francisco).

Eventually his love for the game became so intense that he decided to buy a team. Naturally, it was the Giants, the "Jints," that he tried to buy. In fact, he tried it for years from 1910 on. But the Giants were really a powerhouse then, and they simply weren't for sale. Alas, what was he to do?

The Colonel couldn't buy the Brooklyn Dodgers because if you are a Giant fan you could never be a Dodger fan, and so he finally decided to give up and shout for the other team in town, the Yankees. The Yankees, then, were little better in Colonel Jake's eyes. They were a perennial second division team in the upstart American League, which the Colonel considered little more than a glorified minor league.

Still, they were a team (of sorts!), and they could be bought. So buy them he did: with partner Cap Huston, the Colonel purchased the Yankees franchise in January 1915, for the unbelievably low amount of $460,000. Today, for that price, you would only get a reserve infielder and a couple of rosin bags! Typical of his activites, the Colonel did nothing half way, and he poured his enthusiasm — and money — into the team.

What he did paid off. To give you a comparison, in the twelve years after 1902 when the Yankees moved to New

York from the Baltimore, they finished:
fourth in 1903
second in 1904
sixth in 1905
second in 1906
fifth in 1907
eighth in 1908
fifth in 1909
second in 1910
sixth in 1911
eighth in 1912
seventh in 1913
seventh in 1914.

In other words, they had never won a pennant and finished in near the bottom of the eight-team division. But it was the Colonel to the rescue. With him pouring tons of money into the team all through the period 1915 to 1920, the Yankees could go nowhere but up. For example, he bought Babe Ruth from the Boston Red Sox in 1919 for $100,000, and also made $300,000 in personal loans to the Red Sox owner. In fact, the Colonel bought a score of players from Boston that were to lead the Yankees to pennant after pennant all during the 1920s.

As a result, the Yankees finished third to the White Sox (Alias Black Sox) and Indians in 1919, third in 1920, and then won their first-ever pennant in 1921, with Babe Ruth hitting an unbelievable 59 home runs and 171 R.B.I.s.

Thus the Yankee tradition of buying the best talent money could buy was begun — with beer money. The Yankee dynasty and years of domination started: in the nineteen-year period from 1921 until Colonel Jake

Ruppert's death in 1939, the Yankees won an unbelievable ten pennants, and seven world series. More important, the Yankee's domination lasted long after the Colonel's death, and long after the Ruppert brewery sold the Yankee team in 1945. The Yankees ruled supreme in the 1940s and 1950s.

So what if? If it had not been for beer money, the Yankees would not have become baseball's team supreme and our national past-time might have been ruled by the Saint Louis Browns! The Browns were the most hapless team in baseball history — winning only one pennant in their fifty-two years of existence. They were so bad that their fans didn't love them, and even their mothers didn't think too highly of them. Then suddenly in 1953, when they moved to Baltimore and became the Orioles, all of Baltimore loved them. But no one loved them more than the Baltimore's George Gunkre Brewing Company, which was later bought by Schaeffer and then by Stroh's. Here is a beer ad that was written for them:

Oh, somewhere in the favored land, the sun is shining bright;
The band is playing somewhere, and somewhere hearts are light.
And somewhere men are laughing, and somewhere children clown.
That somewhere, friend, is Baltimore.
The Browns have come to town!

What If? Number 2

For our second "what if?" I will head to "the queen city of the Hudson": Poughkeepsie, New York. Until the completion of the Crozon Aqueduct in 1842, which brought pure and fresh water from the Catskills, New York city's water supply was suspect — at best. Beer brewed with it often left a lot to be desired. As a result, a lot of the beer New Yorkers drank from the mid- to late-1800s came from up the Hudson River. Yonkers, Dobbs Ferry, New Burgh, Kingston, Poughkeepsie, Hudson, Albany and Troy all had sizable breweries that helped supply the Big Apple's beer needs in the nineteenth century.

Poughkeepsie's Eagle — or Vassar — Brewery was one of the more important ones. Founded by James Vassar in 1797, the brewery grew to considerable prominence under the direction of his son Matthew, who took over leadership in 1810 following James' death. Matthew enlarged the brewery in 1810, and again in 1836. By mid-century, Matthew was brewing 20,000 barrels a year. Today, this is pretty much a microbrewery, but then it was a major.

However, by mid-century Matthew's interests were straying from the brewery; he had loftier — more noble, if you will — goals in mind. Gradually those goals settled down to one: the founding of a college for women. In 1861, he chartered Vassar Female College for Women. In the first year, 353 women enrolled. Vassar, who was childless, called them "my 300 daughters." Six years later, in 1867, the name was changed to its present day Vassar College.

Matthew died just a year later in 1868, but long after even his brewery went to the happy, hoppy hunting ground in 1896, his name still lives on. In fact, there is a still-recited poem that goes something like this:

And so you see, for old V.C
Our love will never fail.

Full well we know
That all we owe
To Matthew Vassar's Ale!

So, our second "what if?" is what if Matthew Vassar and his beer money — actually ale money — hadn't founded Vassar College? I will take a moment to read a letter I received from Dixie Sheridan, Vassar's press secretary:

> Dear Mr. Anderson:
> In reply to your letter of April 16 and the theme of your speech ... let me begin by saying that if Matthew Vassar had not founded Vassar College, we would not this year have celebrated the 125th anniversary of the college. Main Building, which first opened its doors to students in 1865, would not have been declared a National Historic Landmark by the U.S. Department of the Interior in the summer of 1986. Answering your specific request for the names of some famous Vassar graduates, I am attaching a list of some well-known people for your consideration. Good luck with your speech.
> Sincerely yours,
> Dixie M. Sheridan

More important than buildings are people. The college that Matthew Vassar founded has helped shape the lives of over 45,000 people who have attended it. And those people, in turn, have helped shape our lives; for example, Edna St. Vincent Millay, a poet; Mrs. Blanchette

(John D.) Rockefeller; Dr. Mary Calderone, a sex education researcher; and Meryl Streep, with her powerful performances in *Out of Africa, Heartburn, Silkwood, The French Lieutenant's Woman*, and *Sophie's Choice*, for which she won an Academy Award.

What If? Number Three

Our third "what if?" starts in early 1940 in Brooklyn, New York. Philip Liebmann, president of Liebmann Breweries, brewers of Rheingold, was called upon by a printing salesman, who wanted to show samples of a new printing process. Among the samples were several shots of a very leggy and very attractive semi-actress, semi-celebrity named Jinx Falkenburg.

The story goes that Philip Liebmann was impressed with the printing process, but was much more impressed with Ms. Falkenburg. As I commented in my book *From Beer to Eternity* , Philip Liebmann had good taste as he would later recount:

"The printing process was revolutionary, but the girl was spectacular. I thought she might be what we needed to promote our beer. We decided to put her under contract for 1940, and hitch our publicity to that face. For the next months she appeared in our advertising, and we were very happy with the results. In 1941, we did it a little differently: we let our dealers pick a girl from a folder bearing pictures of a couple of dozen beauties."

Then in 1942, Liebmann let the public do the selecting. That year, there were 200,000 votes cast for the Miss

Will Anderson

Rheingold girl; by the late 1950s, the Miss Rheingold contest pulled in well over 20 million votes. It was the second most voted election in America; only the presidential election drew more votes, which, of course, is held only every fourth year!

It was an unbelievable event all along the East coast and especially around New York. I can clearly recall as a kid stuffing the ballot box at Louie's supermarket in Ardsley, New York, for my favorite, hoping that maybe someday, somehow, she would personally repay me.

The amazing thing about the Miss Rheingold contest was that it almost paid to lose. The winner got a very nice chunk of money, a super fancy wardrobe, and was treated like a queen for a year. But then she became so associated with Rheingold beer, that it became very difficult for her to get any other type of modeling or acting work after her year of being Miss Rheingold was over.

If a girl lost, however, she got all the exposure of the election and the campaigning, but she didn't become forever associated with beer. At least three losing contestants got that exposure and then went on to greater fame and glory. The first of these was Tippi Hedren, who lost the 1953 election. She went on to star in the Alfred Hitchcock films, *The Birds* and *Marnie*.

Hope Lange was the second loser who became a winner. Less than three years after losing the 1954 election, Miss Lange was a Hollywood regular, appearing in *Bus Stop* in 1956, *Peyton Place* in 1957, *The Young Lions* in 1958, *Pocketful Of Miracles* in 1961, and *Love Is A Baseball* in 1963. She won a pair of emmies for her role in television's "The Ghost and Mrs. Muir."

The last losing Miss Rheingold contestant to go on to

bigger and better things is Diane Baker. She lost in the 1957 and moved quickly into movie roles. Her debut was in *The Diary of Anne Frank* in 1959, followed by *Journey to the Center of the Earth* in 1959, *Nine Hours to Rama* in 1963, *The Prize* in 1963, and *Mirage* in 1965.

Earlier I said there are three prominent actresses who were helped by Miss Rheingold contestant exposure. I stated it that way — "known" — because there may have been a fourth: a losing contestant in the 1949 election named Arlene Dahlman. Did she — as Arlene Dahl — go on to considerable success in such films as *Three Little Words, Woman's World*, and *Wicked As They Come?* I don't know.

So, what if Philip Liebmann hadn't taken a fancy to Jinx Falkenburg? Not only would East-coast America not have had one of its greatest spectacles from 1940 to 1965, but we probably would be without the acting skills of Tippi Hedren, Hope Lange, Diane Baker, and Arlene Dahl.

Our Culture's Effect on Beer

Let's reverse this premise: we have been talking about how beer has affected our culture and history. Just for fun, let's take a much shorter look at how our culture and history have affected beerdom.

Who knows where Henry Wadsworth Longfellow was born and raised? Portland, Maine. The main thing is that if Henry Wadsworth Longfellow had not decided to immortalize Paul Revere's ride in 1875, we would not have one of our better American beers right now. Do you remember this great poem from *Tales of a Wayside Inn?*

"Listen, my children, and you shall hear of the midnight ride of Paul Revere. On the eighteenth of April, in seventy-five, hardly a man is now alive who remembers that famous day and year."

What does this have to do with beer? Fritz Maytag decided to beat the bicentennial rush in 1976 by brewing up a very special ale to commemorate Paul Revere's famous ride. He wanted it to be an ale because New England is — or was — ale country, and in 1975, he developed and introduced Liberty Ale.

What is the moral of all of this? That beer has influenced -- and generally been good to -- America in ways we might not otherwise realize. So, let's take a minute and give a round of applause to Colonel Jake, Matthew Vassar, and Philip Liebmann and the Miss Rheingold girls.

Will Anderson has been researching and collecting beer lore and breweriana for twenty-five years. He has published six books on this subject, including Beer USA *and* From Beer to Eternity. *He is the cofounder of the Eastern Coast Breweriana Association.*

14.
Brewing in Your Environment
Suiting Your Methods to Your Means

Geoffrey Larson
Chinook Alaskan Brewing Company,
Juneau, Alaska

I want to talk with you today about the environment in which you brew and suiting your brewing methods to it. Every brewing environment is different, and yet, every brewery has some sort of relationship to other breweries. We all think we have some unique problems because they are ours, but in fact, other breweries have some of the same difficulties. I believe that the main difference is in the approach, which is dictated by varying environments.

For example, when you talk about pitching yeast into unfermented wort, the yeast's ability to do its job depends largely on the brewer's ability to set the stage, no matter whether he is a homebrewer or commercial brewer. Setting the stage takes knowing technically how to provide the proper environment. It also takes introspection and knowing what you expect from a beer. When the beer is in its final form, how it tastes, compared with how you would like it to taste, gives you an indication of your true expectations. You have to have a desire for a specific product, you have to attempt to produce it, and then the innovations you create will do one thing: increase its

quality. But all this leads
back to knowing your environment.

In Alaska, we have some
seemingly unique problems.
For one thing, Alaska is so
remote that many of the
beers available there are
inherently old — both *older*
and sometimes *pathetically
old*. This is especially true of
imported beers. Breweries
try to keep a fair turn on
their products, but in talking
to distributors, you hear sto-

Geoffrey Larson

ries like, "We had a shipment that was nine days past due.
Where could we ship it? To Alaska."

The Alaskan consumer has virtually no fresh beers,
which on one hand is an advantage to our brewery. This
fact spawned a fundamental movement toward homebrewing in Alaska; making your own beer is about the
only way you can get a fresh product. What we are doing
with our brewery is presenting fresh beer to the consumer.
The disadvantage of having only stale beer available is
that when people think of an import beer — and the
quality associated with that genre — they are so used to
the skunky aroma or cardboardy taste that they don't
notice them as defects.

That is a somewhat facetious statement. In general,
Alaskans travel a lot. It is cheaper for them to go to Hawaii
than to Seattle, and in Hawaii, they are exposed to many
different beers. We felt that there is indeed a niche in

Geoffrey Larson

Alaska that we could fill with a brewery emphasizing beer freshness and variety.

My background was in chemical engineering — designing and installing alcohol plants. My partner was an accountant, so a brewery seemed like a reasonable endeavor for us. We had aspirations of getting the brewery going overnight or in three years at the outside, but the nucleation of the idea was about seven years, during which time we learned a lot about our environment — both the brewhouse and the marketplace. That time proved to be very important to us.

It took time for us to come up to speed, and also it took time for the people who were inherently involved in the brewery to come up to speed. We talked to the distributors and retailers we would need to deal with since Alaskan law prohibits a brewery from selling directly to the public. We talked to sewer and water people who were concerned about the amount of waste the brewery would generate.

We talked to legislators about impending laws; to zoning officials; to building inspectors; and to alcohol abuse agencies. In Alaska, there is an awareness of alcohol abuse. It gets grim out in the bush, and cabin fever is a real problem that can be compounded by drinking. In talking to Mothers Against Drunk Drivers and Bartenders Against Drunk Drivers, they became aware that we were going to produce a high-quality product that would cost more than usual beer and that was less likely to be abused. This mutual education laid the foundation for a nice smooth transition from planning to production.

The name of our company, Chinook Alaskan Brewing Company, is indigenous to the Northwest. It is the name of an Indian tribe, a mountain wind, and also a king salmon. It was the trading language of the Hudson Bay outfitters, and included seven different Indian dialects. We chose the name because it is both regional in nature and specific and unique to our locale. The word Chinook was used by two tribes indigenous to southwest Alaska, where our brewery is located in Juneau. The terrain of Juneau is mountains juxtaposed to the ocean, hence the name Chinook was appropriate.

Juneau is surrounded by an ice field, and since the ice field is our water source, we have the big advantage of having pre-aged water — by 10,000 years! It is good water for brewing. It gave us total flexibility in formulating and designing our beers as we wanted them, but it presented other difficulties. Glacial advances and recessions are seasonal, resulting in a lot of turbidity in the water. We had to put in filtration simply to control the turbidity.

Back in 1907, brewers had an abundance of cold, both in the ocean, which was 38 to 43 degrees F, and also in streams, which were 38 to 40 degrees F. Hence the Alt Style of brewing was used, which is a cold fermentation of an ale. Our water comes into our brewery at 35 degrees F, at a pressure of ninety pounds per square inch. No plumbing in any city, including ours, is guaranteed safe for anything over seventy pounds. So everyone on city water has to sign a waiver. The high pressure and cold water, however, give us a lot of advantages.

When we started to learn about our environment, we tapped many sources of information. For one, we tapped Alaska's history, which is profound. There were forty-eight breweries in Alaska before Prohibition, and a few that started afterwards that met ill-fate. One, Prinz Brau, located in Anchorage, had a 100,000-barrel capacity, and

and had to capture 14 percent of the market share just to break even.

In researching this topic, we discovered recipes from many old breweries. Alaska has a lot of living history. It became a state in 1959, and its pioneer days were in the 1930s and '40s. We spoke to many of the people involved in brewing then, and they were able to relate specific facts about old-time brewing. One important fact underlaid all the recipes we found: heavy original gravities, probably due to people's high caloric needs in the harsh, Alaskan climate. We decided that if earlier pioneers preferred those beers, the pioneers of today would, too.

We researched several old Alaskan brew recipes through the historical society. We coined our recipe after one used by the Douglas City Brewing Company. It was dated 1907 and called for crystal and pale malts and Saaz hops. At this point, we brew only one beer — an alt-style, although we also found recipes for a porter and a pale beer.

In a microbrewery, you need to consider the quality and consistency of the product. Our grind is inspected three or four times during the grinding operation. We don't want too fine a grind that will cause a long lautering; we don't want too coarse a grind that will hinder extraction.

We have a three-vessel brewhouse that includes a mash tun, brewkettle, and lauter tun. The waste we generate in brewing causes its own problems. There aren't any pig farmers in Juneau, so the spent grains have no use. It is a shame to see them go down the drain, but that is how we have to get rid of them. We had to make the city sewage people aware that this was going to be the case. It so happened that because of its abundance of rainfall each year, Juneau doesn't have enough Biology Oxygen Demand in its sewage treatment plants, and was happy to get the waste grains.

We lightly filter our products. Another consideration we had with our environment is that because of dense, widely separated population centers, we were going to have to ship long distances. Most of Alaska's population lives along the coast, and cities are separated by vast amounts of wilderness. We didn't want the tendency for autolized yeast if we were talking about bottle conditioning. Also haze can be one unstable aspect of the finished product. Yet, we had to keep in mind that filtration can strip the beer, so we wanted to minimize filtering. Throughout the brewing operation, we uphold the biological integrity of the brewery and the beer to the utmost. We don't want to have to depend on filtration to give us a sterile product.

Brewhouse cleanliness is pretty fundamental, but even then you must know your brewhouse environment. In Alaska, bottled products are more or less the only way into the market; there isn't much draft beer. It is a developing market that is just evolving to point where keg products can be utilized. When we began, we had to supply our beer in the format that the public and the license holders were used to.

We clean everything. Any day when we feel really good about the stability of our product, we plate the floor. Between pedicoccus and lactobacillus, there are enemies underfoot and all around. If you don't watch them, they will bite you. There are many ways you can get your bottles "sterile," but one fundamental way is by using your rinse track and analyzing how your washing mechanisms are performing.

We have a forty-spout Meyer filler. It had just come out of an operation where it filled 400 bottles a minute, seven days a week, twenty-four hours a day. We use it four hours a week, at a relatively slow rate. The difficulty is that even though we can get it down to fifty bottles per minute by feeding bottles slowly. Again, you have to know your environment. You want the beer to go into the bottle very quickly.

As for clean-up, for every four hours we run the bottling line, we put sixteen hours into prepping. We lube the line, but also we clean it. Beer stones and caustic stones, if left, are deposits that build up to porous surfaces that are hard to sanitize.

Kegging is a market we are trying to develop, and it is actually doing better than we ever expected. I think it gets back to the fact that Alaskans travel a lot. Bars everywhere else in the U.S. offer a draft option. Now, 25 percent of our production — about ten barrels a week — is in kegs. We believe that amount will double or triple in the next eighteen months.

We use an English racking arm that required some modification. The kegs are filled to the brim to evacuate the air and prevent oxygenation. When the beer spills out, we start the bunging operation. On a hard day, bunging is my favorite job; I give them a couple of extra whacks for good measure.

Some breweries have rodent or insect problems. We don't have those; we have *ursus major*, in other words, bear. We have an infestation of bears that want opportunistic meals. They are herbivores, and what they want is malt.

One thing you must know about your environment is whether your packaging is appropriate for your marketplace. In talking to shippers, we asked for their size parameters for packaging. Juneau is landlocked, so beer can't be driven to its destination. It has to be boated or flown in. Our beer is shipped out by ferry and float-planes to bush communities, so we needed to find out how our product would be handled in that situation.

The ferry system that connects most of the southeast, south central and central area is the main transportation for our beer. Shipping by ferries isn't as expensive as flying, but it has a tendency for breakage and loss. We had to use packaging that offers protection. We use brown bottles in cardboard six-packs to protect our product.

We also talked to bar owners who told us their needs and wants. We were interested in using long-neck bottles. Long-necks are a little bit heavier-gauge glass, which would have helped us prevent breakage in shipping. But bars in Ketchikan and Fairbanks don't serve long-necks because they can be used as a weapon. The long neck is literally a handle for the bottle to be used as a club. Had we not known that, we would have excluded ourselves from relatively large markets. Instead, we use a bottle with shoulders.

Alaskans have a lot of pride, especially for local products, and we wanted to tap it. To do this, we had to be very aware of the specific needs of the market — of our environment. So I leave you with the thought that whether you are a homebrewer considering the likes and dislikes of your friends, or a commercial brewer trying to establish a market for your product, the best thing you can do is know your environment.

Q: How much did you spend on your brewery?

GL: Total capitalization was $500,000, including the bottling line. That makes us about fifty/fifty equity to debt. We lease our facility with the option for long-term tenancy or purchase. We did, however, have to make renovations to the building.

Q: What is your brewhouse size?

GL: Brew length is ten barrels.

Q: What is the shelf price of your beer?

GL: We got a real education in determining our shelf price. When I think of a 25 percent markup, I think of 1.25 times the cost. That is not the way it works in Alaska; a 25 percent markup is divided by 0.75, which is equivalent to multiplying by 1.33. You have to be aware of how markup is figured. If you are looking at trying to target a specific price range with your product, you may be way overpriced.

In Alaska, prices for import beers range from $4.25 to $12 a six-pack. Our beer is priced at $6.50 a six-pack, which was at the mean of the import costs when we did our market study.

Budweiser is the largest selling beer in Alaska, with a 50 percent market share. The second place is Rainier in the southeast. Up north, second is Miller. The price of these is probably about $3.25. When we did our market research, we were looking to price our beer against products similar to ours.

There is a tremendous fluctuation in the economy of Alaska. It has been called a "third-world country" in terms of being a raw materials producer. There isn't much manufacturing within the state, which causes difficulties. The infrastructure for shipping is very crude, and for us to

be able to get our product to market and service it takes
more effort than we ever anticipated.

Q: Do you market only in Alaska?

GL: Yes, at this time. Right now, we are only in
southeast Alaska, and our immediate goal is to be
throughout our region of the state, which is approximately 600 miles by 100 miles.

Q: Did your research about your end user pan out?

GL: You can market study anything to death. Our
market study was basically beating the pavement, talking
to bar owners and taking surveys to get a feel for what the
market was about. What was surprising was the support
we have gotten from our local economy. With the down-
turned economy and also the need for diversity in Alaska,
we have experienced a lot of public acceptance for our
product. Still, we have only been on the market for six
months — a mere honeymoon. Everyone will try us
initially, and where our drinkers will come from remains
to be seen.

The population in Alaska is very sparse. There are
only 490,000 people in the state. That is a very small
market, and so we are looking for saturation.

*Geoffrey Larson is president of Chinook Alaskan
Brewing and Bottling Company in Douglas (Juneau),
Alaska. Geoff received his B.S. in chemical engineering
from the University of Maryland and went to work designing and installing alcohol processing plants for a small
manufacturing firm. He moved to Alaska in 1982 and
worked with a mining company for two years before
starting the microbrewery. The Chinook Alskan Brewery*

and Bottling Company sold its first beer on December 28, 1986. The brewery's Chinook Alaskan Amber Beer took third place in the Great American Beer Festival in the Consumer Preference Poll.

The staff preps thousands of commercial and homebrewed beers.

15.
Classic Lager Beer
The Lager Family and Its Sub-Categories

Charles Hiigel
San Luis Obispo, California

I have a different perspective on beer from most speakers at this conference. I am a member of the American Homebrewers Association, and a regular reader of *zymugry* Magazine, but it is because I am a beer lover, not a beer brewer. As the manager of Spike's Restaurant in San Luis Obispo, California, it is my job to spread that enthusiam to customers. The idea is that the more customers I can convert to being beer connoisseurs, the more will become regulars — and regulars are our bread and butter. I have gotten a little carried away with that since it seems that my goals for educating consumers are more ambitious than any I have seen except for the AHA.

In my estimation, lagers seem to be a style of beer that homebrewers don't brew nearly enough. As a commercial beer enthusiast, it is my job to know the beers on the market and how they taste. I have observed that imported lager beers are almost invariably stale — although I like them on the continent of Europe. So if you are not happy with the amount of flavor in the fresh lagers you get in the United States, and you are not happy with the stale lagers from Europe, then you have to brew your own, or support a microbrewery that brews a good lager.

Although I originally planned to speak about lagers, I really want to talk about why we should categorize beer at all, because as soon as you categorize beer, you find that there are very good beers that do not exactly fit the description. In my consumer education courses, I teach a five-week

Charles Hiigel

intensive seminar called "Advanced Introduction to Beer Appreciation." In this class, we sample eighteen beers a night — no two of which are the same style. Ultimately, we taste seventy-five or eighty different beers. What I am trying to teach people is how to identify different styles of beer. I don't worry about the brand listed on the bottle, such as a German Pilsner; I do worry that the beer is a good example of the style I am trying to explain.

I find that the more a person knows about beer, the less he worries about the categorization of beers. From my perspective on the front line of consumer education, the best way I can teach our customers about beer is to write a couple of paragraphs about beer styles on a table menu that shows a map of the world and a short, nontechnical description of the brewing process. I also do one-night-stand beer tastings, where we go through sixteen different styles of beer, and the in-depth class I mentioned before.

Finally, I put on a beer festival for the local symphony, at which I serve imported beers arranged according to beer styles.

The bottom line of what I am trying to teach is that any attempt to categorize beer is an attempt to create a set of expectations before you take the first sip. By categorizing a beer, your enjoyment of that beer may very often be dependent on your mind set, before you even take the first sip. Yet, it is my experience that if you are surprised by a beer, more often than not, you will be disappointed. For example, if you are in the mood for beer "A," and you get beer "B," you will generally not like beer "B."

My job, then, in serving a beer to a customer is to orient the beer to match his mood, or vice versa. If I can read his mood, I can suggest a beer I think he will like. I may have all of ten seconds to this since I am serving a lot of beers, so I have become good at describing beers in ten words or less.

When I train waitresses, I tell them that if a customer doesn't like the beer they served him, it is not the beer's fault. It isn't the customer's fault, either. It is our fault. For example, we list forty beers on Spike's "Around the World" card. A guy walks in, obviously at the end of a bicycle ride. He plops down, slaps his card on the table, and notices that he hasn't yet tried Number 39. He says to the waitress, "I need a Number 39." Never mind that Number 39 is Theakston's Old Peculier.

In this case, it is the waitress's job to suggest that it is not the right time for Old Peculier. If the customer drank Old Peculier on a cold, foggy night for his third beer, he would probably like it. But after a long bike ride, he wouldn't like it, and would appreciate the fact that the

A View of the World from SPIKE'S PLACE

INCLUDING
• All American Brewing Cities
• All Foreign Cities exporting Beer to California, in recent memory.

DRAWN BY CHARLES HUGEL 1985

Charles Hiigel

waitress knew enough to steer him away from it. The point is, it is the same beer and the same customer, but the customer's mood is what makes the difference. The customer (or the waitress) needs to have the beer knowledge to think, "An Old Ale. Hmmmmmm, that's not what's needed right now." Categorization is the factor that will allow you to pick the beer that fits the mood you are in.

When I was asked to describe lager beer variations for *zymurgy* magazine, the first thing I noticed was the category Continental Light Lagers. In almost all of my beer tastings, I have started with describing the differences between Continental Light Lagers. I was pleased to see that American Pilsener had been separated out as a category. That is a subject of some controversy among people, some of whom say that American Pilsener is an inferior, watered-down, weak version of the real thing from Czechoslovakia. I suggest that it is, rather, a completely separate beer, simply because it is brewed with different ingredients than are the Continental Light Lagers. The use of adjuncts is a standard characteristic of the American Pilsener style.

Expectations When Drinking Beer

It is more important to note, however, that these two styles are drank for different reasons, and that is the best reason to categorize beer. If you sit down at Spike's and know that you are going to have three beers, and you have both Budweiser and Dortmunder Union left on your "Around the World" list, obviously your first beer on a hot day should be the Budweiser. If it is cool outside, your first beer should be the Dortmunder Union. The Dormunder

Union may not be a good first beer, but it is a logical step, once your thirst has been quenched with a cold one, to enjoy the bitterness of the Dortmunder Union. Again, you must meet the needs of your mood.

We don't always have the opportunity to do this. You may decide that you are in the mood for a certain beer, but all you have in your fridge is what is left of a homebrew you didn't like, or a Cooper Stout you ignored because you had to drink the lager before it went stale. If you don't have the choice of beers to match your mood, however, you can change your mood to match the beer. If you are a little more open-minded than the average person, you can begin to appreciate a good beer — even one you weren't expecting — after the second or third sip.

There comes the problem of trying to categorize a beer that has the general characteristics of a style but uses ingredients from a certain nationality. An example is Pale Ale. The classic example of this style is Burton-on-Trent, with its bitter head. Then in the United States, you get a beer of roughly the same alcohol content, such as Sierra Nevada Pale Ale, with a somewhat dominant hop flavor and about the same color. They are both called Pale Ale, yet the two beers bear very little resemblance to each other. I believe we are forced to come up with sub-categories for such beers.

When I describe the lager beer style, I use German lagers for discussion. People sometimes complain that I don't discuss Japanese beer, Australian beer, South American beer, Mexican beer. I tell them that you have to go back to the classic example to find the beers that are accepted as the originals of their types; other beers are a derivative of them. That is an unfair statement, because you could, as a homebrewer, decide to brew a German Stout Pilsener or a Danish Stout Pilsener using Cascade hops, which wouldn't be true to type. The hops would become a significant part of the beer's flavor, and yet that beer would be a legitimate sub-category of the Danish Stout Pilsener.

Why do microbrewers brew lager beer? In many cases, it is their beer of choice, based on the fact that they really like German beers, as I do. They crave correct German beers and don't get to Germany very often. Another reason is marketing. I know one brewer, for example, who conducted a market study in his area. The word "lager" kept coming up as a word that sounded good to potential customers' ears — even more than the words "Pilsener" or "beer." The word "ale" was locked out.

So this brewer decided to open a lager fermentation brewery, even with the extra expense of refrigeration and space requirements. In fact, the brewery has equal amounts of footage devoted to brewing and drinking. But the beer he brewed didn't necessarily taste like a lager. It was top-fermented, with the fruity, estery taste associated with an ale. He also is brewing a beer called "amber" and one called "porter," and he is working on another called "stout." The bottom line is that "porter" and "stout" sound good to his customers.

Porter is becoming a commonly used word to describe microbrewed beer. We recently held a festival of California beers and the name "porter" cropped up from several different breweries. In some cases, the same fermentation process is used for beers called "porter" and beers called "lager." They both taste good, but one may be misnamed.

What these do is create an expectation they can't match. So the consumer has to realign his thinking, and say, "This is a good beer, although I was expecting a porter."

Besides correct description, another way of matching the consumer's expectation to the beer is in the presentation of the beer. This is taken for granted by most brewpubs. In California, I am very disturbed to see the English pint glass, or the American sixteen-ounce Martini mixer, being used to present all English beer. I have seen people pouring lagers and wheat beers into them. Fortunately, I have never seen barley wine served in English pint glasses!

The glass that holds a beer decrees a certain expectation. When you are served a beer in a pint glass, you drink it as you would a pint — with a fast, vertical motion of the elbow. When I don't have time to describe a beer to someone, I can reorient his expectations by serving it in an unusual glass. At Spike's we serve some beers in brandy snifters; for example, Gouden Carolus from Belgium, an aged beer with a strong, fruity flavor and a strong sourness from fermentation. If that same beer were purchased at the liquor store, the person might be attracted by the bottle, taste the beer, and pour it down the sink. If you are not expecting its distinctive taste, it is just plain bizarre.

On the other hand, I can serve this beer in a brandy snifter, pour it for the customer, make a big deal out of it, and the snifter immediately announces that there is something different about this beer. The customer thinks, "Maybe I am supposed to smell it before I drink it. Or maybe I am supposed to sip it like I would a brandy."

About 95 percent of the people who have Carolus served in this manner say that it is their favorite on our list. It is the same beer as in the liquor store, but with a different set of expectations.

Continental Light Lagers

There is quite a wide range of variations in the style called Continental Light Lager. If you were German, you would know this, but as a homebrewer, you should research it. The reason for drinking an American Pilsener is the way it *feels*, not so much the way it tastes. That is a very important distinction: when you grab a cold one and wash it down over your palate, you feel the cold all the way down. You say, "That tastes good," but you are using the wrong word. It *feels* good. You really couldn't taste anything at the temperature you just drank it, and it wasn't very full-flavored anyway.

The point is, there are different reasons for drinking beer. I will separate out four different categories, none of them Pilsner Urquell.

Heineken

The first is Heineken, which is representative of "Danish Pilsener." Those words are a tribute to Carlsberg, which has historical significance in the development of lager fermentation. It also is more imitated worldwide than is Pilsner Urquell. Perhaps we could say that all beers trace their roots to Carlsberg. In fact, what most beers are shooting for is a well-balanced flavor between a Budweiser and Pilsner Urquell. This is what could be

Charles Hiigel

called a "normal beer." I try to convince people that the American beer that commands such a large marketshare in the U.S. is not at all "normal," but is a specialized brew for a special mood: hot weather and ballgames.

Heineken is "normal," however, in that no one flavor stands out. In imported beer, the dominant flavor may be old-age or light damage. I have heard it said that if you want to make your beer taste imported, don't let it out of your brewery for four months. You shouldn't be able to identify any one flavor in Heineken because all the flavors are present in equal value. It is light in color, not too heavy nor light in body, and of normal alcohol strength.

Warsteiner

The second example, Warsteiner, is of the German Pilsener style, which I tend to separate from Pilsner Urquell. Americans, when they say Pilsener, usually mean Pilsner Urquell and city beers from Central Germany. I want to point out that categorizing beers by nationality doesn't work because then all German beers would fall into the same group. Most restaurants do list all German beers together, when Pilseners should be listed separately, with ambers, lagers, dark lagers, and bocks in other separate categories, no matter what country they come from. For example, it is easier for me to understand why Danish beer and Bremen (northern Germany) beers are related much more to each other than to a Munich. It is much easier to see how a Munich beer might be a closer relative to a Pilsener beer or a Vienna beer. After sampling all the German variations on lager, I always finish with a Pilsner Urquell, because then people can immediately realize that all the imitators of Pilsner Urquell have missed the mark entirely.

Please notice that in a German Pilsener the accent is on bitterness; it is not at all balanced. It may have the same color as the Danish-style Pilsener, and roughly the same strength, but it is definitely unbalanced in the direction of bitterness. There is a good reason for that. It is desirable before eating. The bitter beers are very good as a warm up to a meal because they make a person hungrier and thirstier. Once you have drunk one German beer, it is very hard not to order a second serving. My suggestion for this beer is that it goes well with the salad course of a meal, or in much the same way that bread is presented before the meal. It serves as the arbiter of things to come. It wakes up the taste buds.

Dortmunder Kronen

A problem comes up in that the beer I use at Spike's to represent my Pilsener category is from Dortmund — Dortmunder Union. It confuses customers to learn that it is not, in fact, a Dortmunder-style beer, but a Pilsener. To clarify that misconception at tastings, I serve Dortmunder Kronen with the idea that it is a much better example of the classic Dortmunder style.

Once again, there is a reason for separating out this beer category: because it goes well with the main course. This is my favorite food beer. The reason? It is less bitter. The Dortmunder Kronen should be well-balanced, that is, not as bitter as a German Pilsener, not as malty as a Munich beer, but a little more alcoholic. You can make the distinction between the very dry, bitter German Pilsener-style and the balanced malt and hops of the Dortmunder.

Muenchner

Finally, Muenchner beer is often not categorized with the Continental Light Lager, but is considered a dark beer. This means dark beer in terms of the everyday beer drinker. But *Muenchner Helles* translates on the Spaten bottle as Munich Light, which means that it is a dark beer brewed without any dark malt.

Essentially, however, a Muenchner has the same characteristics you are looking for in a dark beer — the same mood, maybe even heavier than some dark beers. Since the Bavarians considered dark beer their everyday beer, dark beers there are not strong, not particularly powerful, and are very enjoyable to drink by the liter. The Bavarians are unique in the fact that they consider the Helles (which means bright, clear) their unusual beer. Whereas Heineken has its normal beer and then its dark, Bavarians have their normal beer and then their Helles.

It is a good idea to separate Muenchner out from other German Pilseners in the category simply because the German breweries themselves do. Spaten also produces a beer called Pils. These two beers look the same and have almost the same gravity, but they are considered two different styles of beer.

The most important characteristic in a Muenchner beer is that the aromatic use of hops has been deemphasized. When you lift a glass of good Bavarian beer — either dark or light — you should smell the grain, just as if you were sticking your hand into a sack of malt. I would describe a Munich beer as one that is best used when the beer is the main course. It is very flavorful, although it is not normally a strong beer, and you can drink it by the liter and still be above the table at the end of the night.

Bock

Bock beer is a category that Americans have tremendous difficulty in understanding. I spend more time explaining bock than any other style. I believe that light-colored bock beers are close relatives to the Spaten Munich beers in terms of the dominance of malt in the aroma. But the bocks are much fuller flavored and intense, and about seven percent alcohol by volume. If you want darker beer, you can go to doublebock.

I highly recommend bock as a desirable beer style for homebrewers because it is very satisfying to people who like a lot of flavor.

In summary, the reason for categorizing beers is because there are different reasons for ordering a beer when you are in different moods. If you have the help of categorization, you can select a beer that will satisfy you.

Charles Hiigel has been the beer manager at Spike's Restaurant in San Luis Obispo, California, for over five years. He holds numerous beer awareness classes, and has become highly experienced in consumer beer education. He is a Recognized Judge under the American Homebrewers Association.

16.

Beer Evaluation Techniques
Getting the Most from Your Beer

Grosvenor Merle-Smith
Association of Brewers, Boulder, Colorado

This year, since we had 2,154 bottles of beer entered
in the National Homebrewers Competition, we judged a
lot of beer. The quality of competition beer this year has
taken a quantum leap over past years. People have asked
me, "Is it really better than last year's beer?" I tell them
that it is better than ever! There has been a critical mass
of information or expertise that clicked all across the
United States and resulted in much better beer.

A number of years ago, we noticed that the beer was
getting better, and as a result, we had to create better
judges. We then started the National Beer Judge Certification Program. In combination with the fact that there
was no universal language for judging, we felt that a
common training forum would standardize judging all
across the country. In essence, however, as homebrewers
we are all judges, so I speak to you not specifically as a
competition judge, but as a homebrewer.

I will take you through the beer evaluation process as
we homebrew judges do it. This will provide you with a
procedure to follow everytime you taste a beer, whether or

Grosvenor Merle-Smith, right, discusses National Homebrew Competition with Charlie Papazian.

not it is in a formal situation. What I hope is that anytime you sit down and taste a beer, you will think about it with regard to these evaluation procedures.

Beer Evaluation

First of all, when you sit down to a beer, you want to know what type it is stylistically. Hopefully, you have in your mind the parameters of the style because you will be tasting the beer in relation to what you already know.

You need to have a good idea of what the brewing procedures are for each style of beer. You need to know the use of all the individual ingredients and how they affect the beer. With this knowledge, you can decipher the characteristics of the beer to further evaluate it.

To be at your best, you must be well-rested, particularly if you will be evaluating beer in a formal tasting. Fatigue makes your assessment of beer much more difficult. When you sit down to judge, you need to pace yourself, and if you quickly go through a dozen beers, you should maintain a sense of freshness throughout.

You should come into a tasting with a clean mouth. A number of factors destroy both your ability to taste and many aspects of your beer. Bacteria in your mouth (living on food particles lodged in your teeth) create a highly acidic condition, which will taint your tasting. Greasy food, oil or lipstick coat your mouth and dull your sense of perception, and they also devastate the head-retention qualities of your beer. For example, if you stick your nose in the foam, it will create a crater and destroy the head on the beer. Approach the job of judging beer by being well groomed.

The room in which the judging will take place should be quiet, cool and well-lit. White tablecloths give a good contrast to beer color, and candles can be used for extra light. There should be no evidence of odors or smoke in the room, and you should refrain from wearing perfume or scented soap. The purpose of these instructions is to give yourself a good, clean foundation so you can perceive the qualities of the beer.

Most of the literature prescribes using a good, beer-clean glass. In a hotel situation, this is next to impossible, so I made the decision, as the director of the National Homebrew Competition, to use a high-grade, clear, hard-plastic cup. As much as anyone disparages the idea of using plastic, it is consistent and fairly free of any alien

odors. If there is any residual plastic aroma, at least it is
consistent throughout the judging.

Before you settle down to judge, be sure you have
writing utensils, score sheets, openers and bread to
cleanse your palate. Dump buckets are a necessary
receptacle for dumping beer and containing foaming beer.

The score sheet has been changed this year to reflect
a different rating system. I also placed aroma evaluation
before the visual aspects of beer. (See pages 40-41 for
sample score sheet.) It seemed like most people were
opening their beers and evaluating aroma before they
judged head retention, etc.

Essentially the score sheet is used to guide you
through an evaluation of a beer using all of your senses. In
our competition, we make the bottles available to the
judges because we feel that you can learn a lot from
opening the beer, seeing it in the bottle, and pouring it.
You can tell if the cap is appropriately put on, and then
when you pour the beer, you can hear how it sounds. The
size of the bubbles also give clue as to how the beer will
taste.

In addition, the score sheet lists "bottle infection," and
having the bottle present allows you to evaluate that. Is
there an infection on the fill-line? Is the yeast fluffy or is
it a tight yeast cake on the bottom? Does the head space
indicate oxidation? The bottle will give you clues to these
questions.

In pouring beer into the glass, I like to flop a dollop of
beer into the bottom of the glass and take a look at whether
it is very carbonated. Once I have a sense of that, I tip the
glass and pour the beer down the side so I don't get
excessive head. If there is not enough head at that point,

to fluff up the head and give some good aromatics.

There are several opinions on the best way to pour beer: straight into the middle or dribbling it down the side. In my opinion, the best way is a combination of the two. An appropriate amount of head is necessary — half an inch to an inch and a half — to take some carbonation out of the beer and release the aromatic volatiles that are important to your initial impression of the beer.

After the beer has been poured, assess the aromatics. Put your nose in the glass and take a good sharp whiff, filling your sinuses. Don't keep sniffing, or your olfactory sense will very quickly become dull. If you need to smell it again after the initial whiff, take a few deep breaths of air, then sniff the beer once more.

In the aroma you want to try to confirm the perceptions you had in mind when you poured it and watched it foam up. If it was excessively carbonated, then perhaps you will smell an infection. Think about the ingredients of the beer. For instance, if you are judging a fruit beer, does the fruit essence come through? Malt? Hops? Is the aroma appropriate for the category? Remember that you are judging for the appropriateness of category and the cleanliness of the technical brewing process. One thing we notice in the competition is that many of the beers could have been brewed cleaner than they were.

Having made that assessment, you have the time to go back and evaluate the appearance. Is the beer clear? Is the color appropriate? How is the head: is it maintaining or dissipating? At this point, you should have a very, very good idea of the individual beer. In fact, I can just about complete the score sheet before I ever actually taste the beer. Then I taste the beer almost to confirm my analysis.

In each step of the way, you make an assessment, and then see whether it leads to the next step in your assessment. Did it fool you? Or does the next step confirm you findings?

Take a fairly good swig of beer and move it around your mouth. You want the beer to contact all the parts of your mouth because your mouth perceives different qualities of flavor in different areas: sweet on the tip of the tongue; salt on the sides; astringent under the tongue; bitter in the back; etc. Pay attention to each of these areas to evaluate the flavor you are tasting. Beer is so complex that you must consciously dwell on each of these possibilities to see if they are present. Is the mouthfeel appropriate to the style? Are the ingredients you taste appropriate? Once you have perceived these flavors, swallow the beer, then think about any lingering aftertastes.

The last thing is, think about your overall impression of the beer. Would you like to continue drinking it? One time, when I was in Mexico, I ran across two fellows sitting in a restaurant drinking bottle after bottle of Pacifico. They were fairly inebriated, and I struck up a conversation and found out they had been there for three days testing the drinkability of Pacifico. They did decide, in fact, that they would serve Pacifico in the restaurant.

Quality and Type of Comments

You should be able to go back, review the score sheets you have completed, and be able to say, "I remember that beer." This is whether you are judging in a competition, or evaluating beer for your own education. In essence, you should create your experience of that beer on the score sheet.

For example, here is a score sheet that rates a beer excellent, with a score of 45. The only comment is, "You're doing everything right. Keep it up." If this was a score sheet for a beer you had judged, you wouldn't even be able to identify which beer it was for. On another score sheet, the comment is, "Cut down on the dark grains." Neither of these say much of anything to the brewer.

A third one says, "It's amazing how clear this beer is. You'd impress any brewmaster." It goes on to say, "This is best-of-show quality. Clean aroma, nice lager characters, nice dense head, excellent, excellent balance. Don't change anything, but if you did, maybe 10 percent more hops would be nice." This doesn't say much about the beer, but it does list this judge's perception of the beer. If you were receiving this evaluation of your beer, you would be a lot more tickled to get this one than either of the first two.

Another says, "Very estery. This is a warm ferment. Has a nice fruity character almost like some Trappist ales. Attractive color, and nice, creamy, small-bubbled head."

A fifth says, "Wow! Heavy hops. This brew has too much residual bitterness. Cut way back on the boiling hops. If you really like hops, use more for finishing. This will reduce the bitterness and hike up the bouquet in the floral, hop-flavored characters. Hops boiled for more than about five minutes rapidly loose these nifty volatiles that I guess you love. Other than that, it's a pretty tasty brew. Try it again."

You still don't have a sense of what that beer was from reading this score sheet, but you have a good understanding of the judge's feelings and why. The important thing here is "why?"

How do judges handle evaluating a bad beer? Here is

a score sheet that says, "Too many harsh flavors. Yeasty, sour. Very red color, not dark enough." The final score was less than 20, which is considered a problem beer.

Another one says, "The clarity is good. Beer has nice fruity, estery qualities. Spikey, banana, clovelike aroma due to warm temperatures for wild yeast or possibly contamination. Also solventlike aroma from warm ferment. Too dark for category. Use lighter malts. Possibly uses sugar; avoid if so. Contaminated. Pay more attention to sanitation. Problems are very definitive. Warm fermentation, sugar, contamination, some oxidation."

Here the judge has made an effort to communicate with the brewer. I don't feel that there was the same effort on the other examples. This judge is genuinely making a heartfelt effort to help the brewer, not putting him on the spot. This should be the feeling you try to convey through your score sheets.

It is important that you judge with humility and respect the brewer who made a great effort to send his beer into a competition. Many brewers are just beginning to brew, and it may be difficult for them to get valuable information. This is your opportunity to give it to them. Assume that the brewer is doing his best. He would probably like to make better beer, but may not know how.

Finally, with regard to formal judging, it is extremely important that both the stewards and the judges make certain that the score sheets are completed. We caught a number this year that had identical numbers for two different beers. Then we had to go back and figure out which was which. Some judges forget to put any numbers on the score sheet.

I want to emphasize that it is very important to keep

Grosvenor Merle-Smith

I want to emphasize that it is very important to keep your speed up when you are judging. Spend five minutes on a beer, for example, finish with it, and move on to the next one. You don't have the time in a formal competition to spend fifteen minutes mulling over each entry.

In closing, I have a word of encouragement for beginning judges. Try not to be too intimidated by the judging process. Beer is extremely complex, and judging beer is a life-long process. If you don't know the reason for a certain characteristic in a beer, don't worry about it; just see if you can find out later. There are many aspects of beer that are notable and identifiable, but no one really knows why they occur. We can't all know all the information. It is important that you make the effort to find out. This will teach you a better vocabulary, and will impress the information on your mind.

A lot of the information I have given you today may seem fairly basic, but it is information we can't hear too much.

Q: How do you maintain your perception from the first beer to the twelfth beer?

GMS: You need to be aware of this, but it doesn't have to be a problem. I will often quickly go through a group of beers, and then go back and see if my feeling about them has changed.

Q: How do you handle serving beers at the correct temperature for the style?

GMS: I usually pull the stouts out of the refrigerator sixty or ninety minutes before I take the others out. In fact, you can let a beer warm up on the table while you judge the others. You may find that the volatiles in certain

Grosvenor Merle-Smith is vice-president of the Association of Brewers of Boulder, Colorado, and serves on the Board of Directors. Director of the AHA National Homebrew Competition for the last three years, he has taught beer evaluation classes and helped create the AHA and Home Wine Beer Trade Association National Beer Judge Certification Program.

17.
Innovations in Brewing Equipment
Inexpensive Ways to Create Your Own

Charlie Olchowski
Frozen Wort, Greenfield, Mass.

About twenty years ago I was dumping my first batch of spoiled beer out of a ceramic crock into a beet patch in my parents' garden. At that time, I didn't realize I would be speaking at a national conference about making beer.

Since those days, a lot of things have happened in homebrewing. This hobby finally became legalized in 1979, and with feverish Californians at the helm, we have come a long way in devising equipment from items found in junkyards and in small-scale commercial applications to make excellent beer. Homebrewers are a group of people trying to make good beer not only for economic reasons, but also for its quality. For this reason, we all have a definite interest in finding easier, better, and more efficient ways of making quality beer.

I brought a few items with me to show you some innovations in brewing equipment, but most of the items in my display were collected from around the Denver area. This goes to show you that many homebrewers nationwide have come up with good ideas, which, in turn, clubs and individuals have improved upon. It is for this reason that

Charlie Olchowski demonstrates innovative homebrewing equipment.

we have made a lot of progress in the last five years in this area. I will run through the brewing process and show you some pieces of equipment that can be of help to you.

To begin the brewing process if you are mashing, water is boiled in a kettle until it is about 170 degrees F for the strike water. The strike water is poured into a cooler that has been equipped with a pipe drain system for draining after the mash. The mashing process goes on for sixty to ninety minutes, depending on the brewer's preference and the type of beer being brewed. At the end of the mash, the wort that has been produced is drained, and then the sparging process begins, at which time a sparging coil or similar device is used.

Charlie Olchowski

Heat Sources for Brewing

I have found that one of the most frequently asked questions concerns how to get the brewing process away from the kitchen stove, to an outside location where the mess won't interfere with the family's cooking. An easy, inexpensive way to get it outside is to use a Coleman two- or three-burner, gasoline-powered camp stove. This provides a wonderful heat source. You must, however, be careful since these stoves generate a lot of heat during a ninety-minute boil. If you set the unit on your driveway, you will soon have an indentation in the asphalt. Be sure to place the stove on concrete, stone or a board to avoid this problem.

But there is an even better source of heat — a junked hot water heater. Hot water heaters, given the quality of water in your area, last for a certain number of years and eventually become "leakers." At that point, the gas company or owner installs a new one, and the leaking heater is junked.

To make a good heater for boiling water or wort, contact the local gas company and get a "leaker." Hire someone to cut the tank away, retaining the bottom burner element and a portion of the housing at an appropriate height to serve as a kettle stand. I have found that most brands of hot water tanks have enough rigidity to hold a fifteen-and-a-half-gallon kettle with no problem. For another idea, Dave Wills in Oregon uses a wheel rim as a base stand for the kettle. He removed a burner unit from a hot-water tank and attached it inside a rim. This makes a very stable and efficient heating unit.

Boiling Kettles

The next question people ask is, what do I boil the water in? Many brewers use enameled stock pots, but the enamel tends to flake off under high heat. Stainless steel is preferable, but rather expensive. There is a way, however, to get an inexpensive stainless steel boiler.

Commercial brewers use stainless steel to keg their product. I am from New England, and the situation may be a little different there from where you live. In Massachusetts, there is a ten-dollar deposit for a beer keg. After a person empties a keg and wants his deposit, he has to have a receipt to get back his ten dollars. If he doesn't have the receipt, the store will not take the keg, and it usually winds up in the junkyard as scrap. Until the day Anheuser-Busch, Miller and other brewers register kegs and put a serial number on them that is actively recorded by the store, I believe the kegs will continue to go to the junkyard. This is a boon to the innovative homebrewer who may wish to permanently " borrow" a keg for the ten-dollar deposit, or go to his favorite junkyard and pick one up for scrap value.

My first display here is a Hoover Universal keg used by Coors. It is almost identical to the Sanky kegs used by Anheuser-Busch and Miller on the East coast (a cylindrical keg with handles built into the top rim). The top has been carefully removed, along with the valve system, to produce a nice fifteen-and-a-half-gallon boiling vessel. In order to quickly bring the water or liquor to a rolling boil, all you need is a wok steam cover or similar item to retain the steam, which helps to steadily raise the temperature.

Glenn Hamburg from Boulder went a step further on his. A fifteen-and-a-half-gallon batch of beer is very heavy, so Glenn had a valve system welded onto the bottom (side) of his keg to drain the wort after it has boiled. The valve has been placed right above the bottom of the vessel to avoid getting much of the trub, hop residue and proteins. If you will notice, the valve has been threaded so it also serves as a connection to a copper sparging coil, which is used to run 170 degrees F water over the mash in his mash tun.

Q: To get maximum heat, where do you place the pot in relation to the flame?

CO: Maximum heat production is just at the tip of the inner gas flame. As you know, a gas flame is "liquid," so placing the kettle at that height above the flame will assure the flow of flame over the kettle bottom to provide and maintain heating efficiency.

This brings to mind another point. If you do use a gas system, please understand that in most places the hot water heater was probably fueled by natural gas, and therefore its orifice is set for use with natural gas. If you want to hook it up to propane, which is what you will be using for a twenty-pound barbecue gas grill, then you must have an orifice designed to burn propane. And vice versa applies, make sure the orifices are compatible to your gas source. The gas company or jobber has these available.

Q: If you want to avoid all that trouble, you can buy a fish fryer or steamer from a company called Brinkman. I bought mine for forty dollars in a sporting goods store, and it puts out 24,000 BTUs. It is designed specifically to be used with propane gas, and also to hold large pots on top of it.

Q: Are the kegs also lined with stainless steel?

CO: Yes. When you go to the junkyard, make sure you get a heavy-gauge stainless steel keg. You may find some aluminum kegs with a plastic liner, but do not use them. It is pretty obvious whether or not the keg is constructed of stainless steel.

Mash/Lauter Tuns

Coolers make perfect mash/lauter tuns. Coleman and Igloo coolers are nice because of their insulating quality. I prefer Coleman coolers because of the rigidity of their exterior steel belt. To adapt them to lauter tuns, use hot-water grade, half-inch plastic or copper pipe. If you don't have the tools to cut copper, have someone cut four tubes about the length of the cooler, make a series of saw-blade-width cuts perpendicular to the length of each tube, and fit them together to form a fork-shaped grid. The fittings can be bought in any hardware store. The cuts on the bottom of the copper act as a drain system.

Buy a cooler that has a drain plug built into the bottom. The outside diameter of common, flexible PVC three-eighths-inch inside diameter syphon hose forms a fairly tight bond with the proper copper fitting in the drain hole of the Coleman Cooler. This results in a nice, tight seal around the drain hose.

The strike water is 165 to 170 degrees F. For a typical batch, it is added to roughly nine pounds of crushed grain. The coolers will hold the mash at 150 degrees F (within two or three degrees) for ninety minutes, providing a fairly stable temperature throughout the process. During a normal ninety-minute mash, I stir only two or three times, and little heat is lost.

Another very nice cooler is the Igloo five-gallon cylindrical cooler that has a drum tap fitting onto the bottom (side). This makes a unique system since a very inexpensive stainless steel steamer (used for steaming vegetables or other food) fits nicely into the bottom to serve as its false bottom. This makes a nice system for producing a five-gallon brew.

My only concern for the use of this cooler system for mashing is the contact with plastic at mashing temperatures. Although all plastic cooler liners are food-grade, there is a possibility that some plastic compounds may find their way into your beer. I have never detected any "plastic" flavors in my beers made in these coolers, but if this concerns you , you will have to devise a stainless steel mashing system.

Lautering Equipment

As I mentioned, one-half-inch copper pipe can be used to make a drain system for your mash/lauter tun. This can be accomplished completely without soldering as the tolerances are close enough so that the tube and fittings will stay together throughout the mash, yet can easily be disassembled to clean after the mash is completed.

Another way to lauter after the mashing session is using a pair of four- or five-gallon food-grade pails from restaurants and doughnut shops. First, drill a number of drain holes in the bottom of one pail with a one-eighth-inch diameter drill. Second, install a drum tap at the very bottom of the second pail. Then fit the pail with the bottom drain-holes into the pail with the drum tap. That system, used in combination with sparging bags, gives a very nice means of sparging the grains.

Roller Mill

Before I leave the brewing process, I must mention that a roller mill is excellent for those of you who want to mash. Most people use a Corona grain mill, and others use a roller mill. If you don't have a roller mill, building one is an excellent club project.

Wort Chillers

Now we will move on to what happens after the boil. Here we are looking for methods of cutting the time it takes to get the wort down to the yeast pitching tempera-ture of about 60 degrees F. A number of people have produced various types of wort chillers or coolers, and for that you can refer to the bibliography I have included.

One bare-bones means is an immersion-type wort chiller. At the end of the boil, after the finishing hops have been added and the trub has begun to settle, this wort chiller is inserted into the kettle itself. Cold water runs through it, thus chilling the wort in the kettle . There is no problem with sterilizing this type of chiller or contami-nating the wort with it because it is being immersed into a batch of beer that is nearly at the boiling temperature of water (212 degrees F). Counterflow wort chillers run the hot wort through a copper coil that is contained in a hose or immersed in a container of cold, flowing water. These work effectively as well, but need to be sterilized before use.

The time it takes to chill a batch of wort is directly proportional to the rate of flow through the wort chiller and the temperature of the water in your area. The water in my area is never above 50 degrees F, so I have a very short time in chilling the wort.

There are a few commercial wort chillers of both immersion and counterflow design on the market. I am familiar with BrewCo's wort chiller, which is a coil contained in plastic housing. I have used it, and because of the water temperature where I live, I have chilled the wort in as little as fifteen minutes.

Kegging

Let's jump forward in the brewing process a few days or a few weeks, depending on your brewing habits, to the bottling procedure. People have really worked hard at trying to minimize the time spent bottling beer. The obvious way is to keg. All kegging systems used by the soda producers and the major breweries can be utilized by amateurs, depending on what kind of investment the brewer wants to make, and what kind of attitude he has about kegging.

In New England, the standard keg for many years was the Golden Gate keg. The one really nice feature about this keg is that it has three access points. There is one on the bottom that is for the product; one on the top that is for the CO_2 source; and a wooden or plastic bung on the side. Depending on what your philosophy is about cleanliness, you can use the bung hole as your access point for sterilizing and filling it. This will require a new bung each time, as you will have to drill out the bung.

One thing to keep in mind with any commercial keg is that when you receive it, it may have high-pressure CO_2 inside. It is **very** important that you vent the keg before you open it. The five-gallon Cornelius (soda) keg is vented fairly easily by pressing the valve on either of the stems. The Golden Gate will require a release valve, which is the piece of hardware you use to attach the CO_2 hose to the top of the keg, to vent the pressure.

In New England about two years ago, Budweiser stopped

Finn Knudsen, director of Coors R&D (left

using the Golden Gate system and went to the Sanky system, which is similar to the Hoover Universal system used by Coors. It also can be used by a homebrewer, but it is more complicated. There is a spring-loaded ball-bearing and a gasket, which can be vented by pressing the ball-bearing to release the pressure. There is a 540-degree spring-steel retainer clip inside the mouth of the one-valve opening, but with a couple of screwdrivers, a homebrewer can remove it. I think you may be able to acquire from a

nd Gil Ortega, supervisor of Coors Pilot Brewery, at the Conference.

brewery or other contact the exact tool used to open the keg.

These are nice kegs because they have only one access point, and because they have been engineered so that all liquid inside flows to the entry point when they are turned upside down. They are parabolic in shape, so that when they are turned upside down to be sterilized and sprayed, they drain well.

Cornelius kegs are very simple to work with, although

there are two different connection fittings. You can purchase these kegs from a good homebrew shop, where you also can obtain CO_2 tanks. In my area, Coca-Cola and Pepsi don't even require a deposit on these Cornelius tanks, so you can "borrow" them from your favorite fastfood restaurant.

When the homebrewer kegs his beer, he treats the keg like one giant bottle: it has to be sterilized and primed. Priming can be done by using one-third to one-half cup of corn sugar per five gallons of beer.

Other Means of Carbonation

I would like to introduce Mike Caldwell, who has designed a system for the collection of natural CO_2 gas produced from yeast fermentation. The CO_2 is then put back into the beer with a special pump he has devised. The CO_2 can be used to carbonate beer, soda or water. It is called the Carbocap Carbonator.

Mike Caldwell

I have here a regular one-liter bottle, which I got for free after I drank the soft drink it contained. Or you can even buy these one- or two-liter bottles very inexpensively. You can see here that I have designed a special cap for this bottle that attaches to a hand pump that pressurizes the CO_2 that I have collected for free. Any time you ferment beer, you produce CO_2 as a byproduct. Why throw it away?

First chill the beer. Just before bottling in these one-

or two-liter bottles, you can exclude the air in the headspace by pressing the bottle. Close the bottle cap firmly. Then, as you operate this little pump, you put CO_2 in the headspace. This way you have stored your beer in a completely CO_2 bathed environment.

When you are ready to drink the beer, use this in-line pump to pressurize it. This way, you can vary the CO_2 content within batches of beer, matching the carbonation level to suit the style of beer. There is no sediment with this method, so if you want to take a batch on a picnic or across town to a friend, there is no cloudiness.

I collect the (byproduct) carbonation after the beginning of fermentation, or I use a very high-yield yeast in any sugar solution to produce the CO_2 I store the CO_2 in foil-type balloons (aluminized mylar), or in used two-liter, plastic, soft-drink bottles. Although my current model doesn't filter the CO_2 before it is added to the beer, I am planning to add an activated charcoal filter that will fit into the front of this unit, and also a micron filter that will eliminate any possibility of contamination.

The cap, which I sell, has a one-way inlet valve and fits a standard one-half-, one- or two-liter soft-drink bottle. The cap has an outlet that attaches to a removable hose that runs to the pump. Once the beer in the bottle is carbonated, the CO_2 will not leak out

The basics are: pressure, reduced temperature of the liquid, and agitation to aid CO_2 absorption into the liquid. You can either shake it or pump it. I just count the number of strokes I pump. I already know the pump-stroke volume, and this allows me to set any CO_2 level I want. For example, here I am carbonating a one-liter bottle with three-volume carbonation — this means I am introducing three-liters of CO_2 into a one-liter bottle. You can add less or more, as you desire.

The nice part of this is that if you drink half the beer in the bottle, you can repressurize the remaining beer. Just give it a couple more pumps of CO_2, and it is recarbonated to its original level.

Charlie Olchowski

I would like to conclude by saying that the junkyard (or natural gas company) located in your own hometown can become the most likely place to find a lot of home-brewing aids. If you are very creative, junked stainless steel coffee machines offer higher volume possibilities for mashing and boiling your wort than any of the vessels I mentioned, and will allow you to produce a much larger batch of beer. All you need is imagination, some inventiveness, and a few tools. This type of innovation by home-brewers has led to higher and higher quality beer being produced in this country, by easier means. Keep up the good work!

References

Roller Mills

"The Roller Mill," *Home Fermenter's Digest,* January 1982, pg. 9.

Mash/Lauter Tun Units

"100% Mashed Barley Brew," *zymurgy*, Summer 1980, pg. 10.

"Mashing Systems and Lautering Vessels," *zymurgy*, Special Issue 1985, pg. 43.

Sparging
"How to Build an Inexpensive Sparging System," *zymurgy*, Spring 1984, pg. 36.

Kettles/Kettle Heaters
"Kettles and Burners," *zymurgy*, Summer 1983, pg. 37.

Wort Chillers
"Al Andrew's Wort Chiller," Home Fermenter's Digest, July 1981, pg. 10.

"Guy Pawson's Wort Cooling Coil," *Home Fermenter's Digest*, August 1981, pg. 19.

"Building Your Own Counterflow Wort Chiller," *zymurgy* Special Issue, 1985, pg. 46.

Kegs/Kegging
"The ABC's of Beermaking Part IV," *Amateur Brewer* #5, pg. 11.

"Home Brew in Draft," *Home Fermenter's Digest,* Nov./ Dec. 1979, pg. 21.

"Home Brew on Tap," *zymurgy*, Winter 1979, pg. 6.

"Build a Tapper System," *Home Fermenter's Digest,* April 1981, pg. 17.

"Homebrew Tapper Systems," *zymurgy*, Summer 1982, pg. 25.

The New, Revised and More Joy of Brewing, Charlie Papazian, 1980, pg. 53 - 57.

"Simple Keg Systems," *zymurgy*, Winter 1986, pg. 19.

The Tapper Newsletter, Volumes 1 and 2, by Andrew's Homebrewing Accessories.

Overview of Components

How to Build a Small Brewery, Bill Owens, 1982 (new edition to be printed).

"How to Build a Ten-Gallon Pilot Brewery," *zymurgy,* Special Issue 1985, pg. 47.

The Complete Joy of Home Brewing, Charlie Papazian, 1984, pg. 241 - 251 and 283 - 287.

Charlie Olchowski is a long-time homebrewer and the owner of the Frozen Wort in Greenfield, Mass. He has given presentations about innovative equipment which has made him popular with homebrewers everywhere.

The beers at the GABF taste so good.

Brewers Publications Books

Beer and Brewing, Volume 6

Beer and Brewing is absolutely useful to professional brewers! Here is info from brewing experts at Siebel, Anheuser-Busch, Anchor Brewery, Coors Brewery, and others. In June 1986, 20 brewers and educators spoke at the National Homebrew Conference. This is a transcription of those talks -- complete with original charts and graphs.

5 1/2 x 8 1/2, 256 pp., illus., softcover $18.95

Brewing Lager Beer

This is the most comprehensive book on decoction mashing that we've seen. Part 1 examines beer ingredients. Part 2 guides you through planning and brewing seven classic lager beers – including recipes. Brewer's tables of info are excellent.

5 1/2 x 8 1/2, 320 pp. index, illus., softcover $12.95

Brewery Operations Volume 3

Brewery Operations deals directly with some of the issues microbrewers and pubbrewers face. Contains 15 chapters of material from some of the finest brewery experts, academics and consultants in the U.S. -- from wort production to marketing, yeast and fermentation to getting money for expansion.

5 1/2 x 8 1/2 180 pp. softcover $23.95

Brewing Mead

Can mead be sold to the American public? Our guess is yes, just as it is in Australia. Meads legendary history is a superb marketing tool. Here are step-by-step recipes and instructions for making this honey-based brew. And its history is included.

5 1/2 x 8 1/2, 208 pp. illus., softcover $9.95

1987 Microbrewers Resource Handbook and Directory

Here are the names, addresses and phone numbers of microbrewers, pubbrewers, suppliers, manufacturers, consultants, and others in the brewing industry, updated for 1987. Every brewer and supplier will find the data in this directory worth every cent of its price.

MRHD also is a step-by-step planning guide for starting a micro- or pub-brewery from concept to finished beer, including a state-by-state listing of legislation.

8 1/2 x 11, 164 pp., illus. $35.00

Shipping is $2.50 per order.

Call in your Credit Card order now to 303-447-0816.
or make check payable to:
Association of Brewers P.O. Box 287, Boulder, CO 80306-0287